Women's Studies Collection Development Policies

A project of the
Collection Development and Bibliography Committee

Women's Studies Section
Association of College and Research Libraries
A Division of the American Library Association

Published by the Association of College and Research Libraries
A Division of the American Library Association
50 East Huron Street
Chicago, IL 60611-2795

ASSOCIATION OF
COLLEGE
& RESEARCH
LIBRARIES

ISBN: 0-8389-7596-8

This publication is printed on recycled acid-free paper.

Printed in the United States of America.

Contents

Introduction

Bernice Lacks, Head of Reference
California State University, Fresno

Over the past several years academic libraries have placed increasing emphasis on developing collection policy statements for all areas of the collection. Budget constraints, and a growing interest in shared resources, underscore the value of having written policies. Women's Studies, a relatively new and evolving interdisciplinary field, presents special challenges in constructing a policy statement.

The ACRL Women's Studies Section Collection Development and Bibliography Committee seeks to assist libraries in meeting that challenge through the publication of this collection of sixteen collection development policies representing a broad range of university libraries. When the Committee sent out a call for policy statements in the spring of 1991, a number of libraries responded with policies that ranged from one to ten pages in length, some in draft form and others well developed detailed statements. The Committee felt there was value in publishing the full range of examples. While many of the statements cover the same categories, they are general or specific about different collection areas. Taken together they form a fairly complete picture of what needs to be considered in the development of a collection policy, and they provide a variety of possible models.

The interdisciplinary nature of Women's Studies, drawing on source materials generated by activism as well as academia, raises important questions in collection development. Acquiring interdisciplinary works is often the responsibility of the Women's Studies selector; however, materials to support Women's Studies scholarship and teaching reach into every traditional discipline. They also overlap with other interdisciplinary areas such as Ethnic Studies and Area Studies. Who is to be responsible for selecting feminist critiques of Philosophy, studies of women in India, autobiographies of prominent literary women? In libraries with a number of subject specialists and designated budget allocations, the responsibilities need to be carefully delineated. Policies of Princeton University and the University of Wisconsin, Madison represent different approaches to this problem.

Collection policies also need to be flexible enough to expand bibliographic networks in order to assure coverage of small press materials and nontraditional formats. Policies which explicitly address this dimension include those of Ohio State University, the University of California, Davis, and the University of Delaware. The description of areas to be collected and the desired collection levels, when the materials do not fit neatly into a few call numbers, presents another major question. Libraries have addressed this in various ways. Some policies use broad general subject categories, some use the Research Libraries Group Conspectus list of LC class numbers, and one library, SUNY Oswego, has used a listing of subject areas from a major bibliography in Women's Studies.

The relationship of the Women's Studies collection to collections elsewhere on campus, in the community, or in the region may also be an important consideration. The policies of Indiana University and the University of Washington describe such relationships. While not a unique phenomenon, Ohio State University's policy is the only one included here from a campus where there is a separate Women's Studies Library.

A number of libraries currently are exploring cooperative loan arrangements and collaborative acquisitions projects. Two examples of cooperative agreements are included here in Appendices A and B and may serve as models for other institutions seeking to develop similar arrangements.

It should be noted that if there is an existing collection development policy within a library, the Women's Studies policy generally follows the format adopted by the institution. For those who are writing policies in libraries which have not adopted a particular form, the 1989 ALA publication *Guide for Written Collection Policy Statements* will be very helpful.

For everyone writing a policy, or revising a policy for Women's Studies, the *RLG Conspectus : Women's Studies*, included here as Appendix C, is an essential tool. Specifically intended for the evaluation of collections, the Conspectus also offers an important contextual framework for the development of policy statements. It outlines the nature of Women's Studies, describes its materials and sources for those materials, and clearly delineates the issues unique to the emerging discipline. Sections of particular interest for those building collections are the Introductory Overview of Women's Studies, and the sections on library materials, scope, and specific LC class numbers. The version of the Conspectus included here consists of the Supplemental Guidelines and a series of subject class lines designed by author Sarah Pritchard for the pilot document. The Conspectus with the RLG worksheets is available from RLG.

The Collection Development and Bibliography Committee of the Women's Studies Section of ACRL wishes to express its appreciation to those libraries who have so generously shared their policies. Our most sincere thanks go also to The Research Libraries Group for permitting the reprinting of the Conspectus for Women's Studies as part of this document.

INDIANA UNIVERSITY LIBRARIES
COLLECTION DEVELOPMENT POLICY
April 1989

COLLECTION: Women's Studies   COLLECTION DEVELOPMENT
                                     LIBRARIAN: Polly Grimshaw

Narrative

1. GENERAL OBJECTIVES AND SUBJECT BOUNDARIES: To collect relevant serials and monographs about women that support and encourage undergraduate and graduate teaching and research relating to women and gender. The interdisciplinary program of Women's Studies includes individual faculty, graduate and undergraduate students who conduct research projects in the major subject areas of Sociology, History, Anthropology, Psychology, Philosophy, Political Science, Economics (including women in the labor force), and Criminal Justice. This also includes biographies and autobiographies of women in these areas.

Subject areas which are not covered by this fund are: Women in Africa, Latin America, Eastern Europe and the Soviet Union; Afro-American and Chicano women; fiction in all languages by women and literary criticism of women in literature (see English, Modern European languages and Comparative Literature). Monographs about women in music, sports, education, journalism, art and religions will be individually evaluated for addition to the graduate collection. Women as authors of research publications (unless it pertains to women) should be evaluated and considered by the pertinent subject or area fund.

2. SCOPE OF COVERAGE: Language: Primarily in English with special attention being given to the pertinent major works in Western European languages. Lesser emphasis is given to Dutch, Flemish, Scandinavian languages, and Italian and Portuguese. Exclusions: The vernacular languages of East Asia, South Asia, and Southeast Asia; the languages of the Middle East; and Slavic and Eastern European languages. See the pertinent area studies collection development policies for the collection levels in these languages. Translations of pertinent research in all languages are considered for purchasing. Chronology: Primarily within the past 300 years. Geography: Comprehensive coverage is given to research on women in the following areas: North America (including Canada), Western Europe (with above language limitations), and Oceania. Limited coverage (level 3) to Asian countries: Japan, China, Korea, Southeast Asia, South Asia and the Middle East. Excluded geographical areas are: Africa, Eastern Europe and the Soviet Union, Latin America and the Caribbean. See the pertinent area studies collection development policies.

3. FORMATS COLLECTED: Monographs, serials (journals, annuals and newsletters), pamphlets and monographs published in a series. Selected dissertations and manuscripts in microfilm (fiche), and proceedings and reports of conferences, symposia, international

congresses, etc. Exclusions: Textbooks, audio visual materials, audio cassettes, data banks and most government publications (see government publications collection policy). Inclusions: Some basic reference books, handbooks, and dictionaries etc. are also purchased for the general collection. Retrospective purchasing is now done on a very selective basis, focusing primarily on titles having to be replaced due to theft, mutilation, or deterioration. The collection is routinely surveyed and evaluated as reprinted monograph and serial titles become available.

4. RELATED COLLECTION DEVELOPMENT POLICIES: Journalism, Business, Folklore, Art, Music, Religion, HPER, Medicine, Education, and Government Publications.

5. OTHER RESOURCES: Research Center for Sex, Gender and Reproduction (Kinsey), Law Library, Education Library, Business Library, Human Relations Area Files and the Political Science Data Laboratory, and the IU School of Medicine Library.

6. LC CLASSIFICATION SCHEDULE:

COLLECTION INTENSITY INDICATORS

The following codes are used in describing existing collection strength (ECS) and current collection intensity (CCI) for the collection development policy's Classed Analysis. In interpreting the ECS/CCI values, it is important to bear these points in mind:

1. These values describe collections or collection policies absolutely, not relatively. They assume therefore a national perspective and a broad cognizance of all facets of collecting.

2. When the value describes existing collection strength, it should relate to national shelflist measurement, reflecting what is actually on the shelves.

3. When the value describes current collecting intensity, it represents actual collecting practices, and not policy, if that policy is being imperfectly observed.

Collection level codes:

0--Out of Scope: The library does not collect in this area.

1--Minimal Level: A subject area in which few selections are made beyond very basic work.

2--Basic Information Level: A collection of up-to-date general materials that serve to introduce and define a subject and to indicate the varieties of information available elsewhere. It may include dictionaries, encyclopedias, access to appropriate bibliographic data bases, selected editions of important works, historical surveys, bibliographies, handbooks, and a few major periodicals in the minimum number that will serve the purpose. A basic information collection is not sufficiently intensive to support any advanced undergraduate or graduate courses or independent study in the subject area involved.

3--<u>Instructional Support Level</u>: A collection that is adequate to support undergraduate and MOST graduate instruction, or sustained independent study; that is, adequate to maintain knowledge of a subject required for limited or generalized purposes, of less than research intensity. It includes a wide range of basic monographs, complete collections of the works of more important writers, selections from the works of secondary writers, a selection of representative journals, access to appropriate non-bibliographic data bases, and the reference tools and fundamental bibliographical apparatus pertaining to the subject.

4--<u>Research Level</u>: A collection that includes the major published source materials required for dissertations and independent research, including materials containing research reporting, new findings, scientific experimental results, and other information useful to researchers. It is intended to include all important reference works and a wide selection of specialized monographs, as well as a very extensive collection of journals and major indexing and abstracting services in the field. Pertinent foreign language materials are included. Older material is retained for historical research.

5--<u>Comprehensive Level</u>: A collection in which a library endeavors, so far as is reasonably possible, to include all significant works of recorded knowledge (publications, manuscripts, other forms), in all applicable languages, for a necessarily defined and limited field. This level of collection intensity is one that maintains a "special collection"; the aim, if not the achievement, is exhaustiveness.

<u>Language Codes</u>:

E--<u>English Language material predominates</u>. Little or no foreign language material is in the collection.

F--<u>Selected foreign language materials included in addition to the English language material</u>.

W--<u>Wide selection of materials in all applicable languages</u>.

Y--<u>Material is primarily in one foreign language</u>. The overall focus is on collecting material in the vernacular of the area.

INDIANA UNIVERSITY LIBRARIES
COLLECTION DEVELOPMENT POLICY
CLASSED ANALYSIS

Women's Studies
May 1989

LC CLASS / (LINE)	DESCRIPTOR	ECS*	CCI#	NOTES
HQ 1101 (WOST 1)	Periodicals. English	2E	3E	
HQ 1102 (WOST 2)	Periodicals. French	1F	2F	
HQ 1103 - 04 (WOST 3)	Periodicals. German & Other	1F	2F	
HQ 1105 - 1111 (WOST 4)	Yearbooks, Congress, Collections	3F	4F	
HQ 1115 (WOST 5)	Dictionaries	00	00	See Reference
HQ 1121 - 1154 (WOST 6)	History	3F	3F	English language 4E
HQ 1161 - 1172 (WOST 7)	Germanic, Latin, Slavic, Muslim, Oriental and Jewish women	3F	3F	
HQ 1180 - 81 (WOST 8)	Study and Teaching	3E	3E	
HQ 1201 - 1233 (WOST 9)	General and Special Aspects	3E	4F	Includes psychology of women, aesthetics
HQ 1236 (WOST 10)	Women and the State	3F	4F	
HQ 1381 (WOST 11)	Women and economics	3E	4E	
HQ 1386 (WOST 12)	Women and literature	3E	4E	i.e.: works on the social relations and problems as affected by literature
HQ 1389 (WOST 13)	Women in art	4E	4E	As a profession only. See also Fine Arts.
HQ 1390 - 91 (WOST 14)	Women in public service	4E	4E	

*ECS = Existing Collection Strength; #CCI = Current Collecting Intensity

LC CLASS / (LINE)	DESCRIPTOR	ECS	CCI	NOTES
HQ 1393 - 95 (WOST 15)	Women and religion	3F	4E	
HQ 1397 (WOST 16)	Women in science and the arts	3E	4F	
HQ 1399 (WOST 17)	Women and civilization	3F	4E	
HQ 1402 - 1439 (WOST 18)	Women in U.S.	3E	4E	See also GPD
HQ 1451 - 1870.5 (WOST 19)	Women in other countries	4E	3F	See also area programs
HQ 1870 - 8 (WOST 20)	Women in communist countries	00	00	See Area Studies Program
HQ 1870.9 (WOST 21)	Women in underdeveloped areas	3E	3F	See also GPD
HQ 1871 - 2030.7 (WOST 22)	Women's clubs	3E	4F	

INTERDISCIPLINARY

LC CLASS / (LINE)	DESCRIPTOR	ECS	CCI	NOTES
BF 105.W6 (WOST 23)	Women philosophers	3F	3F	
BJ 1609 (WOST 24)	Ethics for women	3E	4E	
BV 676 (WOST 25)	Women as ministers	2E	2E	
BV 1300 - 1395 (WOST 26)	Religious societies for women	3F	4E	Includes YWCA
D-DU (WOST 27)	History of Women in Specific Countries	3E	3F	
GN 59.W6 (WOST 28)	Anthrometry - women	3F	4E	
GN 67.5 (WOST 29)	Body dimensions and proportions	4F	3E	
GN 479.5 (WOST 30)	Ethnology - matriarchy	4F	4F	
GN 479.7 (WOST 31)	Sex roles - women	4F	4F	See also HQ 1075

LC CLASS / (LINE)	DESCRIPTOR	ECS	CCI	NOTES
GN 480 - 480.65 (WOST 32)	Domestic groups	3E	4F	
N 482.1 - 5 (WOST 33)	Life cycle - birth	3E	4E	
GN 484.4 - 7 (WOST 34)	Life cycle - marriage	3E	3E	
GT 1720 (WOST 35)	Costume - women	3E	3F	See also Folklore
GT 2520 (WOST 36)	Customs relating to women	4F	4F	
HD 3423 (WOST 37)	Cooperative guilds for women	3E	4F	
HD 6050 - 6620.7 (WOST 38)	Women in industry including working mothers	4F	4F	See also GPD and Business
HG 8801 (WOST 39)	Life insurance for women	4E	4E	
HN 49.W6 (WOST 40)	Women in social reform	3E	4F	
HQ 27.5 (WOST 41)	Sexual behavior and attitudes - girls	3E	4E	
HQ 29 (WOST 42)	Sexual behavior and attitudes - Women	3E	4F	
HQ 46 (WOST 43)	Sex instruction and ethics for women	3E	3E	
HQ 51 (WOST 44)	Sex instruction and ethics for girls	2E	2E	See also Education.
RQ 75.2 (WOST 45)	Lesbians	2E	3F	
HQ 101 - 440.7 (WOST 46)	Prostitution	3F	3F	
HQ 759 - 759.6 (WOST 47)	Wives - mothers	3E	4E	
HQ 760 - 767.7 (WOST 48)	Family planning, birth control and abortion	2E	4E	See pertinent #'s in obstetrics and gynecology, IU Medical Center, & GPD.

LC CLASS / (LINE)	DESCRIPTOR	ECS	CCI	NOTES
HQ 798 (WOST 49)	Adolescence	3F	3E	See also Sociology and Education
HQ 800 (WOST 50)	Celibacy and single women	3E	4E	
HQ 801 - 805 (WOST 51)	Courtship, dating, matrimony	2E	4E	
HQ 806 (WOST 52)	Adultery	3E	3E	
HQ 809 - 809.3 (WOST 53)	Family Violence	2E	4E	For wife abuse see HV 6626
HQ 811 - 960.7 (WOST 54)	Divorce	3E	2E	
HQ 961 - 967 (WOST 55)	Free love	3F	3F	
HQ 981 - 997 (WOST 56)	Polygamy and Polyandry	4F	4F	See also Anthropology and Sociology
HQ 1001-1043 (WOST 57)	The state and marriage	4E	4E	See also Sociology
HQ 1058 (WOST 58)	Widows	4E	4E	
HQ 1075 (WOST 59)	Sex roles	3E	4F	See also GN 479.7
HQ 1101 (WOST 60)	Feminism	3E	4F	
HQ 1121 (WOST 61)	History	3E	4E	
HQ 1127 (WOST 62)	Ancient	3E	4E	
HQ 1143 (WOST 63)	Medieval	3E	4E	
HQ 1150 (WOST 64)	Modern	3E	3F	
HS 853 (WOST 65)	Women in free masonry	2F	2E	

LC CLASS / (LINE)	DESCRIPTOR	ECS	CCI	NOTES
HS 3348 -3365 (WOST 66)	Girl's societies	4E	3E	
HV 541 (WOST 67)	Women and charity	4E	4F	
HV 879 (WOST 68)	Girl's protection, assistance, etc.	3F	3E	
HV 1442 - 48 (WOST 69)	Assistance for women	3E	4E	
HV 5137 (WOST 70)	Women and alcohol	2F	4E	
HV 5203 - 475) (WOST 71)	Women and temperance reform	4E	4E	
HV 5824.W6 (WOST 72)	Drugs and women	2E	4F	
HV 6046 (WOST 73)	Women offenders	4F	4F	
HV 6250.4 (W65) (WOST 74)	Women as victims of crime	4F	4F	See also GPD
HV 6558 (WOST 75)	Rape	4F	4F	
HV 6626 (WOST 76)	Wife abuse	2E	4E	
HV 700.5 (WOST 77)	Assistance of unmarried mothers	3E	3E	
HV 8738 (WOST 78)	Prisons for women	4E	4E	
HX 546 (WOST 79)	Communism/socialism and women	3E	4F	
JK 1881 - 1911 (WOST 80)	Women suffrage in U.S.	4E	4E	See also GPD
JN 976 - 985 (WOST 81)	Women suffrage in G. B.	2E	4E	
JX 1965 (WOST 82)	Women and the peace movement	4E	4F	

LC CLASS / (LINE)	DESCRIPTOR	ECS	CCI	NOTES
K 118.W6 (WOST 83)	Women lawyers	2E	4E	See also GPD
K 644 (WOST 84)	Civil law and women	3E	4F	
K 670 - 709 (WOST 85)	Domestic relations, family law	2E	2E	See also Law Library
K 1824 (WOST 86)	Labor laws and women	3E	4F	See also GPD
K3230.W6 (WOST 87)	Consitutional law and women	3E	4E	See also GPD
K 3297 (WOST 88)	Suffrage - women	4E	4F	
LB 2843.W7 (WOST 89)	Salaries of women teachers	2E	2E	
LC 212.8 - .863 (WOST 90)	Sex discrimination in education	2E	4E	See also Education
LC 1401 - 2571 (WOST 91)	Education of women	4E	4F	
N 8354 (WOST 92)	Women as artists	2E	2F	
NA 1997 (WOST 93)	Women as architects	2E	3F	
ND 38 (WOST 94)	Biography women painters	00	00	
PN 1590 (WOST 95)	Women in Performing Arts	00	4E	See also Music and Cinema
PN 4872 (WOST 96)	Biographies of women	4E	4F	
PN 4879 (WOST 97)	Women's magazines	3E	4F	
Q 130 (WOST 98)	Women in science	3E	4F	
R 692 (WOST 99)	Women in medicine	3E	4F	

LC CLASS / (LINE)	DESCRIPTOR	ECS	CCI	NOTES
RA 778 (WOST100)	Women and personal health	3E	3E	
RC 451.4.W6 (WOST101)	Women and psychiatry	3E	4E	See also GPD and Education
RC 560.F7 (WOST102)	Frigidity and women	2F	3E	
RC 560.153 (WOST103)	Incest and women	3F	3F	See also GPD
RC 560.R36 (WOST104)	Rape and women	3E	3E	
RC 963.6.W65 (WOST105)	Women and industrial medicine	3F	3E	
S 494.5.A4 (WOST106)	Women in agriculture	2E	4F	See also GPD and Business
U 750 (WOST107)	Military wives	1E	3E	
UA 565.W6 (WOST108)	Women's service corps	3E	3E	See also GPD
Z 7961 - 7965 (WOST109)	Bibliographies	4F	4F	Subject specific only. See also Reference for general.

WOMEN'S STUDIES LIBRARY
COLLECTION DEVELOPMENT POLICY
DRAFT
THE OHIO STATE UNIVERSITY

II.   Subject/Location Library Statements

   A.   Women on campus first requested a separate women's
        studies library in 1972. Women's studies courses had
        been in existence at Ohio State University for 2 years
        and the momentum of the women's movement was rapidly
        increasing. Plans were in the works to establish a
        feminist academic program and the need for a library
        to support the goals of this program was recognized
        from the outset. In response to these developments a
        small group of librarians, led by Beth McNeer, began
        publishing a biweekly annotated list of pertinent
        titles owned by the Ohio State libraries entitled
        Women Are Human. Donations from sororities and various
        women's organizations initially funded a small
        collection of books and periodicals within the
        Undergraduate Library. The collection continued in
        this ad hoc manner for a few years but with the
        creation of the Office of Women's Studies in 1975, the
        desire for a separate library greatly intensified.
        Through the combined efforts of the new Office and
        library administration this goal was partially
        realized with the appointment of Abby Kratz as half-
        time women's studies librarian in October 1976. The
        materials budget for 1976/77 was $3,590 and the
        collection included 1,463 cataloged volumes, 38
        serial titles, and 148 microforms. The following
        year a separate library became a reality when the
        collection moved to the second floor of the
        Main Library in August 1977. The first year's
        circulation figure was 3,539.

        By 1980 the Office of Women's Studies had become
        the Center for Women's Studies and the Library had
        become an official department library. The budget
        was close to $8,000, the collection consisted of
        almost 4,000 cataloged volumes, 64 serial titles,
        and 569 microforms. Circulation had mushroomed to
        9,747. Women Are Human evolved into Women's Studies
        Review, the first publication in the U.S. devoted
        solely to reviews of books by and about women. In
        1988 Women's Studies Review and the Center's Sojourner
        combined to become Feminisms. Responsibility for
        publication transfered to the Center though library
        staff still serve on the editorial board and
        contribute articles and book reviews.

By 1990/91 an M.A. in Women's Studies had been
approved by the university. The Library had moved to
a new area of the second floor and had become an
offical unit of Main Library. The collection
contained over 15,000 cataloged volumes, 100 serial
titles, over 1,600 microforms, and nearly 3,000
uncataloged pamphlets in a subject vertical file.

The purpose of the Women's Studies Library is
to provide library services that support the
curricular and research needs of the Center for
Women's Studies and other courses or projects that
focus on women or contain a component on gender.

1. Clientele
     Primary clientele are the 12 core and 33
     affiliate faculty in the Center For Women's
     Studies and graduate and undergraduate students in
     the women's studies program. There are 26
     graduate associates, 17 of which are members of
     the first official class of the new M.A. program,
     and 135 undergraduate majors and minors. Over
     3,000 students enrolled in women's studies
     classes in 1990/91.
     Secondary constituents are faculty and students
     in other departments that offer courses or conduct
     research on women and Ohio State organizations
     devoted to women such as Women In Development,
     Women Student Services, and the Rape Education and
     Prevention Program. More than 20 departments
     offer courses on women and over 100 faculty
     are engaged in research on women.
     The Anthropology, Black Studies, Communication,
     English, Psychology, and Sociology departments
     actively encourage graduate work in women's
     studies. The History Department offers a PhD. in
     women's history and the Education Department
     offers a PhD. with an emphasis on gender and
     education. Ohio State's undergraduate curriculum
     was recently revised to include components on
     race, gender, and class so the secondary
     constituency has grown considerably.
     Tertiary constituents are non-Ohio State faculty,
     scholars, and students in women's studies,
     non-Ohio State organizations devoted to women, and
     the community at large.
2. Curriculum
     Ohio State offers a B.A in women's studies
     with an emphasis in humanities or social sciences,
     an M.A. in Women's Studies, and a one-of-a-kind
     PhD. with an emphasis in women's studies.

3. Research programs
   Research programs are particularly strong in African American and African women's studies, feminist theory, American history, literary and visual arts, social and political movements, public policy, women's heath and sexuality, Latin American women, and women in development.

4. Special or topical collections
   Nineteenth century women's periodicals, archives of women's liberation movement newsletters and newspapers from the late 1960's and 1970's, and ERA newsletters are all special collections.

5. Other
   Not applicable.

6. Participation of faculty in collection development
   Library staff, selected faculty, and student representatives serve on the Center's Library and Publication Committee. Individual faculty also submit suggestions or requests for purchase.

B. The nature of the subject literature is highly inter-disciplinary and encompasses both scholarship and feminist activism. In response to growing demand, numerous academic and trade publishers have increased the number of women's studies titles they offer particularly in the areas of theory, diversity of experience, and international women. However, alternative publishers and small presses devoted to materials by, about, and for women still provide important coverage of trends and developments in women's issues and feminist thought. The majority of titles published are in the humanities and social sciences but inroads are being made in the sciences and applied fields.

C. The collection contains materials in all LC classification areas. It is especially strong in history and the social sciences, language and literature, philosophy, psychology, and religion, and health issues. Weaknesses include agriculture, technology, military and naval sciences, natural sciences, music, foreign language materials. Care is taken to reflect various perspectives whether theoretical schools of feminism or experiences of diverse women, for example, lesbians, women of color, working class women, aged women, disabled women, international women, and women in development.

Emphasis is on feminist materials and materials that describe the conditions, experiences, and contributions of women in multi-cultural contexts.

1. Reference
    The reference collection consists of unique holdings of women's studies titles and judicious duplication of interdisciplinary titles and bibliographies. The Information Services Department (ISD), located on the first floor of Main Library, houses such supplementary materials as government documents, the census, and other statistical sources.

2. Monographs
    Approximately 15,000 volumes support a basically interdisciplinary curriculum and make up the largest component of the collection. The vast majority are academic titles though highly selective popular titles are also included.

3. Serials
    The collection consists of roughly 100 unique titles that includes the major scholarly journals in women's studies as well as a few popular magazines. Women's Studies Abstracts, Studies On Women Abstracts, and Women's Studies Index are the main tools of access. However, indexing is necessarily not a requirement for acquisition, retention, or preservation since many serials important to the development of the field are not indexed by the traditional sources. Women's Studies serials are the only OSU holdings presently listed in the Ohio Union List of Serials.

4. Intentionally unclassified collections
    Not applicable.

5. Special segmented non-LC collections
    Not applicable.

6. Cataloging backlog collections
    Foreign or small press materials not on OCLC make up the bulk of the backlog.

7. Others as appropriate
    A pamphlet file of materials on perennially popular subjects and extensive microfilm holdings complete the collection. Included in the approximately 60 sets of microform are major collections like the Gerritsen Collection of Women's History, the National Woman's Party Papers,

the <u>Woman's</u> <u>International League For Peace and</u> <u>Freedom Papers</u>, and the <u>Papers of the Women's Trade</u> <u>Union League and Its Principal Leaders</u>. Other sets consist of papers of individuals or families like Eleanor Roosevelt and the Blackwell family, archives and records of various women's organizations like the American Association of University Women, and many historical journals like <u>Godey's Lady Book</u>, <u>The Progressive Woman</u>, <u>The Ladder</u>, and <u>Herstory</u>. All sets of microform and their printed guides are cataloged and accessible through the library catalog. They are housed in the microforms section of ISD on the first floor of the library.

D. Scope of the historical and current collecting activity
   1. The historical and current collecting activity generally reflects the development, growth, and needs of the Center for Women's Studies program. Subject concentrations are as follows:

   Social Sciences and history include the economic conditions of women, women and work, sociology of women, discrimination, sex roles, sexism, lesbianism, women in marriage and the family, women and politics, feminism and women's movements, women's studies, women's rights, women's history, women in the United States, women in development, international women, women's welfare, crimes against women, violence against women, female offenders, and women in the criminal justice system.

   Language and literature encompass women in the mass media, communication, sexism in the media, sexism in language, women in popular culture, feminist criticism and theory, women in film, feminist film theory and criticism, and women in national literatures particularly American and English. (The emphasis in national literatures is on feminist authors, poetry and fiction of authors taught in women's studies classes, and anthologies published by feminist presses).

   Philosophy, psychology, and religion include feminist philosophy, feminist criticism of major philosophers and schools of philosophy, women philosophers, the psychology of women, feminist criticism of major psychologists and schools of psychology, women psychologists, women and religion, feminist theology, women and the church, women in various religious traditions particularly Christianity, Judaism, Islam, witchcraft, and goddess.

   Health encompasses women in medicine and women's mental and physical health issues such as depression, counseling, breast cancer, osteroporosis, pregnancy,

child birth, eating disorders, and reproductive
technologies.
  Women's issues and feminist theory in political
science, law, education, geography/anthropology,
fine arts, agriculture, technology, the natural
sciences, the military and naval sciences, and
music are also collected to a lesser extent. This
is due to few women's studies materials published
in these subjects or strong department library
holdings.

2. Access
    LCS (Library Control System), Ohio State's online
    catalog, provides the main access to the collection.

3. Subjects excluded
    Materials merely by or about women that do not
    contribute to the academic study of gender are
    excluded from the women's studies collection.

4. Ohio State libraries overlaps and "underlaps"/gaps
     Because of the interdisciplinary nature of the
    women's studies literature, overlaps with other
    subject collections and departmental libraries
    are inevitable. The most notable ones occur
    with the Education/Psychology Library, the Social
    Work Library, the Black Studies Library, and the Human
    Ecology Library. Duplication of important titles or
    titles in subject areas of high demand is often necessary
    to meet the needs of various constituencies. This has
    been especially true since the revised curriculum
    includes a gender component. Bibliographers confer
    about titles in "gray" areas that do not justify
    more than one copy. The area studies libraries
    traditionally collect literature in languages other
    than English and translations of these. The Women's
    Studies Library traditionally does not collect in
    the areas of music and the fine arts. The
    collections in these areas are usually limited to
    women and popular music, general feminist music theory
    and criticism, selected women composers, feminist
    art theory and criticism, images of women in art,
    selected feminist artists, and gift books on various
    other women artists.
     Gaps in the Ohio State libraries' collection include
    medical ethics particularly in areas such as genetic
    counseling and reproductive technologies and
    international women's literature in English.

5.   Language coverage
      The collection is basically comprised of materials
in the English language. However, feminist theory
and original data in other languages, primarily
French, Spanish, German, and Italian, are selectively
collected to support the M.A. program.

6.   Chronological period covered
      The collection is not limited by chronological
period.

7.   Chronological publication period covered
      The collection is not limited by chronological
publication period.

8.   Geographical area covered
      The collection is international in coverage.

9.   Specific materials solicited as gifts
      Gifts are solicited for out-of-print, missing,
or duplication of heavily used materials.

10.   Other materials
       Not applicable.

11.   Not collected or collected and handled in a special
       manner
       AV materials and pulp fiction are not collected.

E.   Related sources pertaining specifically to the subject/
location collection.

1.   Ohio State resources outside the Libraries
      The Center For Teaching Excellence collects
films, videos, and other AV materials in women's
studies.

2.   Local resources
      The Ohio Historical Society collects historical
materials on women in Ohio. The Women's
Information Center collects materials of interest
to the state legislature.

3.   Cooperative agreements
      Not applicable.

4.   External memberships
      Not applicable.

5.   Online access
      Not applicable.

F. General future collection plans and specific weaknesses
    that need to be addressed
        The Women's Studies Library will continue to focus on
    materials on international women and build on the strengths
    of the collection. Weak areas will be reinforced as
    publishing patterns change and materials in the sciences
    and applied fields become available. Groundwork has already
    been laid for buying foreign language materials with
    advice from the area studies librarians. Cooperation
    with department libraries regarding new journals that
    overlap collections is also necessary as subscription
    prices continue to climb.
        Buying patterns have been adjusted to accomodate the
    gender, race, and class components of the revised curriculum
    and support the new M.A. program in women's studies. It
    is quite feasible that a PhD. program in women's studies
    will be developed by the end of the decade. Technology
    has finally "discovered" the field of women's studies
    and at least one CD-ROM product is presently being developed.
    The Library must begin to prepare for these important
    developments now. Space is aproblem but selective transfers
    and careful weeding will hopefully see us through until the
    new storage unit is built.

G. Detailed subject, collection intensity, and language
    coverage will be delineated in accordance with the North
    Americans Collections Inventory Project (NCIP/Conspectus)
    1. This portion of the policy will be completed as a
        separate project subsequent to completion of the
        written collection policies
    2. This project will act as a verification process
        and review of the written collection policy

H. Appendices specific to the subject/location
        Wilde/Stein Development Fund for the purchase
        of lesbian and gay materials

        Submitted by Linda A. Krikos
                     Head, Women's Studies Library

Ohio University Libraries

COLLECTION DEVELOPMENT POLICY FOR WOMEN STUDIES

STATEMENT OF PURPOSE

To provide guidelines for the acquisition of library material in Women Studies.

At present, the Women Studies program is a certificate program available as an option in any undergraduate or graduate degree program offered by the University. Courses which earn credit toward the Women's Studies certificate include courses in the departments of Anthropology, Afro American Studies, English, History, Health and Physical Education and Sports, Interpersonal Communication, Linguistics, Political Science, Sociology, and Zoology.

SELECTION GUIDELINES

Material will be selected in order to:
    1. support/supplement the recognized Women Studies courses presently offered
    2. provide findings and facilitate research of the female experience historically and currently, locally, regionally, and internationally
    3. correct the imbalance of information that has been available on women and their accomplishments, concerns, and viewpoints.
    4. support and encourage equity in all areas of the University by making available legal studies, research, and models for change

As more, and more varied material on women and gender issues continues becoming available, it is expected that most such material will be purchased by the appropriate academic/subject departments. The Women Studies Bibliographer will seek to keep the academic/subject areas informed about relevant material of mutual interest. Cooperative effort is necesary to increase the library's ability to deal with the growing research and interest in the study of women, gender roles, and related issues.

Women Studies funds will purchase interdisciplinary material which does not fit a single subject area, and which brings an important feminist viewpoint or offers new or rediscovered information about women, or provides access to such information.

Material purchased will not be limited to any time period or geographic area, but material providing a broad perspective will generally be preferred over that dealing with an area of very limited interest. Efforts will be made to ensure the collection reflects the experience of women of all races, and many nations.

Material will be purchased in print or microform depending on availability, cost, and expected use.

WOMEN'S STUDIES

I. GENERAL COLLECTING GUIDELINES

A. General Purpose

To support teaching and research, at the undergraduate and graduate
levels and beyond, on the role of women in various societies and the
changing nature of social and political relationships between men and
women; to provide information to the general university community
about these topics. Particular concern about this area rests with the
inter-departmental Women's Studies Program, but the materials are also
of interest to the faculty and students in History, Sociology, Anthropology, Economics, Politics, Psychology, American Studies, Classics,
Literature, Biology, Art, Music, Theatre and Industrial Relations.

B. Subjects Excluded

Medical, anatomical or physiological works (see Biology); literary
works by, or criticism of, women authors (collected by the various
literature and area studies selectors); marriage and the family (see
Sociology).

C. Overlap With Other Collections Or Subjects: Division of Responsibility

Because of the interdisciplinary nature of Women's Studies, there is
considerable overlap with other subjects, particulary Sociology,
Psychology, History, Economics, literature and area studies. As a
practical matter, due to the very limited amount of money allocated
for Women's Studies, materials with pertinence to other fields are
routed to the appropriate selectors for consideration in relation to
their policies. Purchases on the Women's Studies budget are normally
those materials not able to be so routed, or those which other
selectors are not willing to fund and which otherwise meet the
criteria of this policy.

D. Languages Collected And Excluded

Emglish is the primary language of collection, with materials in
other major European languages acquired on a selective basis,
primarily when an English translation is unavailable. Materials in
non-Roman alphabets are not acquired.

E. Geographical Limits

No region or country is excluded, but emphasis is placed on the
United States

-2-

F. Chronological Limits

Emphasis is placed on contemporary persons and current developments, but material is collected relating to all historical periods.

G. Retrospective Acquisition

Because Women's Studies is a new field of study at Princeton, considerable retrospective buying, especially of original source material, is necessary to compensate for previous inactivity in this area.

H. Types Of Material Collected And Excluded

Collected: monographs; serials; government documents; pamphlets; microforms; manuscripts; dissertations from U.S. institutions, textbooks.

Excluded: audio-visual materials, foreign dissertation; juvenile material.

I. Other Factors

None.

II. SUBJECTS AND COLLECTING LEVELS

History Of Women, Including Feminist Movement

United States	Collecting Level
Colonial period	3
18th and 19 centuries	3
20th century	4
Other countries	2
Biography	3
Psychology of women	3
Women in literature and art	4
Women and economic issues	3
Women and social issues	4
Women in public service	3
Women and religion	3
Careers and occupations of women	4
Education of women	4
Women's organizations	2

Attatachment to Women's Studies Collection Development Policy

II. SUBJECTS AND COLLECTING LEVELS

These subject and collecting levels reflect what is bought on the women's studies fund. The overlap with other statements part is meant to reflect what is bought for the library in this field and to reflect the level at which the women's studies selector checks for materials that might have been missed in the normal selection process. These are then routed to other selectors or purchased.

	Collecting Level
Feminism, with an emphasis on United States	4
Lesbian studies	3
Gender studies (overlap with Politics level)	3
Women and music	2
Women and religion	3
Women and science and technology	2
Women and the performing arts, mass media	2

Overlap with other statements

History of Women	History at	4
Biography	DR collects at	4
Psychology of women	Psychology at	4
Women in art and literature	Art and literature	4
Women and economic issues	Economics and IR at	4
Women and social issues	Sociology & History at	4
Women and politics and law	Politics & Law	4
Women and religion	Religion most at	4
Careers and occupations of women	Economics & IR at	4
Education of women	Education at	4
Women's organizations	Sociology at	3
Women and biology and medicine	Biology & Psychology	3 & 4

DRAFT
WOMEN'S STUDIES
COLLECTION DEVELOPMENT POLICY

Nancy Seale Osborne
SUNY College at Oswego
Oswego NY 13126
(315) 341-3567

CURRICULUM OVERVIEW

Women's Studies comprises the academic study of women and gender across all subjects; feminism as a multi-faceted, multicultural international movement addressing a wide range of social, political, and economic issues; and feminist critique and theory not only related to women but to general academic subjects and contemporary concerns. Women's studies is highly interdisciplinary and draws on a variety of sources and methods. Although regarded first as a social science, Women's Studies has made contributions in all domains from the narrow study of women as an aspect of traditional categories of scholarship, to a feminist critique of knowledge that calls for a restructuring of all intellectual analysis.

Penfield Library utilizes two approaches to collection development in Women's Studies: the development of a separate, cohesive body of feminist theory and research about women, and the transformation of the mainstream curriculum through integrating theory and research into individual disciplines.

A letter of intent to institute the Women's Studies program at SUNY College at Oswego was written in 1973. The Women's Studies Program Minor was approved in 1977-78. Its interdisciplinary and multicultural structure provides the opportunity for students to choose Women's Studies courses in political science, history, psychology, sociology/anthropology, physical education, philosophy, communication studies, English, art, counseling and psychological services. The current human diversity/global general education curriculum requirement, as well as selected longterm, established courses, integrate gender studies into the overall college curriculum.

COLLECTION DEVELOPMENT GUIDELINES

a. <u>Languages</u>: English will be the primary language of the collection; some works, particularly in international literature, will be purchased by the Foreign Language area selector. Cooperation between and among collection development area selectors is essential to the success of an interdisciplinary area like Women's Studies.

b. <u>Chronological Guidelines</u>: A substantive amount of the collection is twentieth century, but due to a strong historical perspective in Women's Studies, all periods are covered.

c. <u>Geographical Guidelines</u>: With the advent of the Human Diversity component of General Education, more materials from other-than-European influence are likely to be purchased. The new Human Diversity Geographical Focus is extremely useful to all area selectors, but for interdisciplinary Women's Studies, it has been and is a vitally important determinant of obtaining multicultural materials.

d. <u>Treatment of subject</u>: The breadth and interdisciplinarity of the field of Women's Studies as it is practiced in the United States is best illustrated by the list of chapter headings in Catherine Loeb, Susan Searing, and Esther Stineman's *Women's Studies: A Recommended Core Bibliography, 1980-1985:*

Anthropology, Cross-Cultural Surveys, and International Studies
Art and Material Culture
Autobiography, Biography, Diaries, Memoirs, and Letters
Business, Economics, and Labor
Education and Pedagogy
Health, Recreation and Physical Education
History
Language and Linguistics
Law

Literature (subdivided into Drama, Essays, History and Criticism,
    Mixed Genres, and Poetry)
Medicine, Health, Sexuality, and Biology
Politics and Political Theory
Psychology
Reference (Audiovisual, Bibliographies, Biographical Materials,
and   General)
Religion and Philosophy
Science, Mathematics, and Technology
Sociology and Social Issues
Sports
Women's Movement and Feminist Theory
Periodicals

Emphasis is on the scholarly; however, selected popular works
are acquired. Historical and survey material are both selected. In
some instances, multiple editions are purchased, but due to the
small budget for this collection development area, only
replacement/enrichment opportunities are taken.

   e. <u>Types of material</u>:
      1. A thorough collection of reference tools: indexes,
bibliographies, directories, almanacs, dictionaries, biographical
works, and works in library science
      2. Current academic and trade publishing: scholarly
monographs, texts, anthologies, fiction and creative writings, and
general or popular works
      3. Serial and monographic works from non-traditional sources:
ephemeral, small press, activist, and ethnic materials
      4. Historical collections in history, science, and social
sciences, treating of women or traditional female concerns or
written by women even if not on the subject of women
      5. Periodicals: academic, activist, literary and popular
magazines (note: this area for Women's Studies is outstandingly
lacking in Penfield Library; the monograph collection has been much
more sustained during Women's Studies development in the past two
decades)
      6. Documents from the United States on public policy, law,
development, health, education, and economics
      7. Working papers, conference papers

8. Non-print resources: films, videotapes, music; access to databases
9. Special Collections: manuscripts, archival materials, photographs, diaries, correspondence, realia

f. <u>Date of publication</u>: Retrospective buying is confined mostly to damaged materials. In some instances duplicate copies are obtained, but due to the limited budget for this interdisciplinary area, this seldom occurs. Current materials are more likely to be ordered in Women's Studies. The field itself is only fifteen years of age; each year brings a proliferation of materials of all qualities and levels of content.

g. <u>Other General Considerations</u>:

1. Students from all other disciplines utilize Women's Studies purchases, all the way from English 102 students and Psychology 100 students, to graduate students in Technology, Education, and Counseling and Psychological Services.

2. Due to the proliferation of Women's Studies resources, many of the small press materials ideal for a strong Women's Studies collection are not purchased. More and more Women's Studies acquisitions are from mainline and university publishing houses like Pergamon and the University of Illinois. Most of the publications indexed in *Women's Studies Abstracts* are not owned by this library. Penfield subscribes to a minimal number of Women's Studies periodicals.

3. The Women's Center has a lending library which includes good books and periodicals.

4. Inasmuch as all disciplines are not covered by Women's Studies faculty, it is imperative that collection development attempt to cover all intellectual bases, even when there are no Women's Studies faculty teaching in a specific discipline.

5. The ratio of monographs to periodicals is woefully inaccurate in comparison to most major library collection

development resource recommendations. The Women's Studies periodical holdings are in fact woefully inadequate.

6. ____% of Interlibrary Loan at Penfield is in the Women's Studies area. The ratio of books to periodicals is not a useful figure, inasmuch as the library has so few periodicals in the Women's Studies area.

7. Online searching in the area of Women's Studies would be especially useful, if it were publicized. This is especially necessary because of the small Women's Studies periodical collection in Penfield. Years of neglect in this area has made Penfield the holder of an excellent monograph collection and the holder of a minimalist periodical collection.

COLLECTION DEVELOPMENT RESOURCES

As in other disciplines, *CHOICE* is a major selecting tool, as is *Books for College Libraries,* third edition. The Women's Studies Librarian periodicals and current bibliographies from the University of Wisconsin are a mandatory source of collection development. *Belles Lettres* and *The Women's Review of Books* are also vitally important. *Building Women's Studies Collections: A Resource Guide,* by Joan Ariel; *Women's Studies: A Recommended Core Bibliography,* by Stineman and Loeb; and *Introduction to Library Research in Women's Studies,* by Susan Searing are all useful. *New Books on Women and Feminism* from the Office of the Women's Studies Librarian at the University of Wisconsin is the most comprehensive continuing bibliography of English-language works in all areas of Women's Studies. *Library Journal* and *Publishers' Weekly* are among the library periodicals which offer some selections for Women's Studies consideration.

The University of Akron

COLLECTION DEVELOPMENT POLICY FOR
THE WOMEN'S STUDIES PROGRAM

SCOPE AND PURPOSE: A library collection in support of the curriculum and research needs of the women's studies program needs to cover the fields of literature, history, politics, business, health, psychology, education, law, and marriage and the family as they relate to women. It should also cover sex roles and women's occupations and professions. The collection draws upon materials in the social sciences, humanities, natural sciences, and fine and applied arts. It is collected at the levels detailed below. The scope is worldwide and from ancient times to present day. The emphasis is on the modern period, particularly the 19th and 20th centuries, collected at the advanced study level, with greater depth on those eras and for the United States and Great Britain which are collected at the research level. The immediate background centuries, the 16th through the 18th, should also be built at the advanced study level for those two countries. Materials for other countries and eras are collected at the initial study level. Support from other departments, whose courses are part of the women's studies certificate curriculum, will have support for those courses in their collection development policies.

CURRICULUM: The women's studies program is an undergraduate interdisciplinary certificate program. There already exist at the university many courses concerned with women which this certificate program uses as electives. There are at present no evident connections among these courses. The certificate program in women's studies articulates and strengthens the connections among courses offered in differing fields, and gives students a coherent background, knowledge and a theoretical framework with which to analyze and evaluate material from varied disciplines. The certificate program in women's studies is also significant for university faculty. With its new emphasis on women's studies, the program becomes a means uniting faculty and community women with similar interests. By encouraging cooperation and interchange across disciplines, it opens up new areas for research. The curriculum involves introduction to women's studies, individual studies of women and, seminar in women's studies. There is also a special topics option. Elective courses in the revised certificate program are existing courses in different colleges. The elective courses are drawn from the social sciences, humanities, fine and applied arts, the College of Education, and the Community and Technical College.

GEOGRAPHICAL COVERAGE: Coverage is worldwide with major emphasis on women in the United States, then England, then Europe and the third world. This is not because the latter areas are of less importance but because there is greater concentration of available courses in the first two areas, especially in literature, the history of women, and the women's movement. The collection should be built at the research level for the United States and Great Britain and at the initial study level for the other areas.

LANGUAGE: English is the only language necessary for the collection.

PERIOD COVERAGE: Coverage is from ancient times through the present day with emphasis on the 20th century. There will be less collected on ancient times. There will be the most on the 19th and 20th centuries because most of the major figures and movements are from those eras. The collection should be built at the advanced study level for the 16th through 20th centuries and at the initial study level for the rest except for 19th and 20th century United States and Great Britain which should be built at the research level.

PUBLICATION TYPES: The following publication types are included: general works, scholarly works, textbooks, collected works, government documents, and research reports. Journals are also included. The collected works are those of individual women, both literary and non-fiction, and the document collections include materials from all areas and times illustrating the lives of women.

FORMATS: Print and audiovisual materials are both acquired. About 95 percent of the materials will be in printed formats.

REMOTE SOURCES: Of the NEOMAL schools which have women's studies programs Oberlin College is the only one with special library resources for women's studies. The existence of that resource does not eliminate our need to collect the resources described in this policy.

EXCLUSIONS: Technical works that deal with medicine for women are not included on this policy, but are acquired under other departmental collection policies.

Revised 12-6-89

UC DAVIS LIBRARY
COLLECTION POLICY STATEMENT

Subject: Women's Studies

Bibliographer: Jane A. Kimball

Degrees Granted at UCD:

A.B.

Collection Size:

HQ   plus materials classified in diverse classifications throughout the social sciences, the humanites, and the arts. Material on biology, physiology, and women's health care classified in Q through R.

Location:

Shields Library
Library Annex
Northern Regional Library Facility

Number of Faculty:

Number of Other Academic Staff: 0.50 FTE

Number of Students: Graduate:

                                Undergraduate: 16

WOMEN'S STUDIES

I. Description of Existing Collection.

Library materials of interest to students and researchers in women's studies are found throughout the Library of Congress classification scheme. Feminism is classified in HQ1101 to HQ2030, and this area contains material central to women's studies. However, materials relating to women may be found in almost every LC class. For example, popular women's periodicals are found in A; psychology and religion as they relate to women in B; history in D, E, and F; anthropology and social customs in G; sociology and work in H; law in J and K; education of women in L; women in the arts and literature in M, N, and P; reproductive biology, physiology, and women's health in Q and R; women in agriculture and technology in S and T; women in the military in U and V; and bibliographic works in the Z classification.

Since women's studies is both academic and activist, the collection contains both mainstream scholarly and academic works published by trade and university presses, and other materials published by specialty presses that represent the diversity of feminist thought.

II. Programmatic Needs and User Constituency Served by the Collection.

The Library's collections on women are used by students and researchers in virtually every campus department and by the general public.

Although there are only 16 Women's Studies majors, the core course Women's Studies 50 is given to 150 students each quarter and has a long waiting list. Most other courses are given as part of the offering of other academic departments. Within the Women's Studies major, there are two areas of concentration. The first, Women and the Humanities, requires courses in Comparative Literature, English, and Linguistics. The second, Gender and Society, allows the student to select among courses in Afro-American Studies, American Studies, Anthropology, Asian American Studies, Chicano Studies, Human Development, Native American Studies, Political Science, Psychology, and Sociology.

III. Current Collecting Guidelines.

a. **Types of Material and Format:** Juvenile materials and introductory textbooks are not ordinarily collected. Hardback editions are purchased whenever possible; however, since many works published by women's presses are issued only in paperback, paperback editions are purchased and bound to make them more durable. Anthologies of previously published material are acquired as appropriate.

   Reference materials and indexes and abstracts are purchased extensively. Serials contain much material that is important in women's studies. Subscriptions to new journals are acquired after careful review by the women's studies bibliographer and, where appropriate after consultation with faculty and with the Women's Resources and Research Center Library. Unpublished theses and dissertations from other institutions are acquired on a selective basis. Expensive microform collections are usually purchased through the University of California Shared Collections and Access Program.

b. **Language Guidelines:** Most material purchased is in English, with English translations of foreign language works acquired whenever possible. Important works in major Western European languages are purchased on a selective basis.

   Materials relating to women that are purchased on other funds; e.g. material in the sciences, are purchased in foreign languages as appropriate to the collecting policies for those disciplines.

c. **Geographical Guidelines:**   The scope of the collection is international, with particular interest in women in developing countries. Material from small presses is predominantly from the United States and Britain because of the language emphasis on English as described in b. above.

d. **Chronological Guidelines:**   Material on women in all periods is collected. Emphasis is placed on changing roles of women and gender in contemporary society.

e. **Dates of Publication:**   Women's Studies is a young discipline, and much feminist scholarship has been produced in the last two decades. Emphasis is on current material, although gaps in holdings of important women authors are filled if material is available. Reprints of early works are often preferred to the original printing because of the acidic content of older book papers.

f. **Other Considerations:**   Since women's studies emerged from and continues to reflect a revolutionary social movement, an effort is made to collect both scholarly materials and those from feminist activists. Materials selected are intended to represent the diversity of feminist perspectives and the richness of women's experiences. Works by and about women outside the mainstream of the interests of the academy, such as lesbians, working-class women, and women of color are collected as are works detailing the struggle of women in traditional societies for equal rights.

Collecting of material in Women's Studies is divided between a diversity of material in the social sciences and material in the arts and literature where works of feminist authors and artists is collected.

On a selective basis, material relating to campus programs such as self-defense for women and rape prevention is acquired for the library's collections.

IV. Other Resources at UC Davis.

The most important source outside Shields Library for materials in Women's Studies is the Women's Resources and Research Center Library in the Memorial Union. Close coordination of library acquisitions between the WRRC Library and Shields insures that the two collections complement rather than compete with each other.

The Minor British Poets Collection in the Department of Special Collections in Shields Library contains works of British women poets from 1789-1972. The Ruth Finney Collection contains the papers of a national reporter for the Scripps-Howard news syndicate from the 1920's to the 1950's. The Avant Garde Poetry Collection contains works of American women poets from 1945 to 1980. The Margaret B. Harrison Collection contains the collected materials of a local woman book binder and paper conservator.

The Law Library contains materials relating to women and the law and to family law.

V. RLG Conspectus Levels.

(All subject subdivisions imply materials about women or of interest to users of Women's Studies materials.)

Existing Collection Strength (ECS); and Current Collecting Intensity (CCI).

	ECS	CCI
Philosophy	2/3	3E
Religion	2/3	2E/3E
Psychology	3	3E
History	3	3F
Anthropology	3	3F
Economics	3	3E
Sociology	3	3E
Feminism	3	3E
Political Science	3	3E
Law (includes holdings of Law Library)	3	3E
Education	2	2/3E
Music	2	2F
Art	2	3F
Linguistics	3	3F
Literature	3	3F
Women in Science	3	3E
Gynecology	4	4F
Psychiatry	4	4F
Technology	3	2E
Military Science	1/2	2E
Subject Bibliography	3	3F

JOAN ARIEL
Women's Studies Librarian
and
Academic Coordinator for Women's Studies

UNIVERSITY OF CALIFORNIA
University Library - Reference
Post Office Box 19557   Area Code 714
Irvine, California 92713   856-4970

UCI LIBRARY

SELECTION POLICY FOR WOMEN'S STUDIES

General Purpose

To support teaching and research through the Ph.D. level and individual faculty or group research at the post-doctoral level. The School of Humanities offers a Humanities Interdisciplinary Major with an Emphasis in Women's Studies. Majors in other disciplines--most often Humanities, Social Sciences, or Social Ecology, but also the sciences--may elect to complete the minor in Women's Studies. Women's Studies and Gender may be an elective field of concentration for the Ph.D. in Humanities, Social Sciences, Comparative Culture, and Social Ecology. The interdisciplinary Focused Research Initiative (FRI) on Women and the Image supports the work of faculty and graduate students in the areas of 1) Gender and Women's Studies; 2) Feminist Theory; and 3) Female/Male Forms of Representation.

Languages

English is preferred. Materials in French and Spanish are purchased within appropriate subject parameters; German language materials on feminist theory, movements, and literature are purchased on a more limited basis. Works in other languages unavailable in English translation are purchased on an extremely selective basis.

Geographical Areas

Major emphasis in on the United States, Latin America, Western Europe and Canada, with signficant interest and coverage in India, Asia, and Third World countries.

Chronological Limits

Current works are emphasized in most subject areas supplemented by major theoretical and historical works regardless of the period in which they were written. On a selective basis, expanded chronological coverage is provided for works in United States and Western European women's history and literature.

Types of Material Collected

Relevant printed materials in hard copy are emphasized. Microform materials are purchased to support Women's History and other subjects areas requiring primary sources. Audiovisual materials are purchased selectively to support campus curriculum and programs.

Types of Material Excluded

Elementary textbooks, handbooks, and manuals are generally excluded.

Other Factors

Women's Studies is inherently interdisciplinary and thus selection crosses and materials are required across many disciplines and programs. Selection, therefore, necessitates cooperation among subject librarians.

Subject and collecting levels (in general call number order)

Women and Philosophy/Religion..D/C

Women and Psychology...C

Ethnic and Minority Women in North America...C

Women and Geography..D

Women/Gender and Anthropology (marriage, sex roles, etc.)......................C

Women and Sport...E

Women and Employment, Labor, Economics..C

Women and Sociology, Family, Sexuality...C

Feminist Theory..B

Women's History & Movements -- United States...B

                 -- Western Europe..B

                 -- Latin America...C

                 -- India..C

                 -- Asia, Africa, Third World................................D

Autobiography, biography, diaries, memoirs, letters..................................C

Women and Politics, Government -- United States..................................C

                      -- Canada...C/B

Women and Law..C

Women and Education...D

Women and Music...D/C

Women in Art..D

Women and Language, Literature and Mass Media

        Greek and Latin Literature...E

        Russian Literature...D

        Asian Literature...C

        Romance Literature (including Latin America)................................C

        English Literature..C/B

        American Literature (United States)...................................B

        African Literature...D

        Feminist Literary Theory/Criticism....................................B

        Performing Arts, Drama, Film..C

        Communication, mass media, sexism, pornography.......................C

Women/Gender and the Sciences...C

Women and Medicine...C

Women and Agriculture...E

Women/Gender and Technology..C

Women and the Military..D/E

Women in Publishing, Library Science, Bibliography.................................C/B

COLLECTING LEVELS

A. <u>Comprehensive Level</u> - a collection that attempts to include all significant works of recorded knowledge for a defined and limited field; the aim is exhaustivenes.

B. <u>Research Level</u> - a collection that supports doctoral and post-doctoral research and requires minimal reliance on inter-library loan; it should include all important reference works, journals, monographs, and major indexing and abstracting services in the field.

C. <u>Advanced Study or Beginning Research Level</u> - a collection that supports graduate and advanced undergraduate course work, or sustained independent study; it should include fundamental works of scholarship, whether monographs or journals, and the reference tools and bibliographical apparatus pertaining to the subject.

D. <u>Teaching or Initial Study Level</u> - a collection adequate to support the undergraduate curriculum; it should include a wide range of basic monographs, complete collections of the more important writers, major journals in the field, and fundamental reference tools and bibliographic apparatus pertaining to the subject.

E. <u>Basic Information Level</u> - a highly selective collection developed to introduce and define a subject falling outside the scope of the curriculum and to indicate the varieties of information available elsewhere; it may include basic reference tools, a few major periodicals and selected editions of important works in the field.

University of California, San Diego
Central University Library
Collection Profile

Subject: WOMEN'S STUDIES

Bibliographer: Susannah Galloway

Degree(s) granted at UCSD: Women's Studies Major
                            (proposed 1991)

Collection size (approx. # volumes): 10,000 volumes (HQ)

Location(s): HQ Section and throughout the collection by
              subject

No. of students: No data available at this time

No. of faculty: 32+

Brief statement of purpose & scope: To support the Women's
Studies Program at UCSD and to meet the undergraduate,
graduate and faculty research and instructional needs in all
disciplines relating to women and gender.

I.   Description of Existing Collection

        A large core collection of Women's Studies
materials is located in the HQ Section of the Central
Library, with a large section of HQ's in the Reference
Collection on the second (main) floor. It represents
approximately 10,000 volumes. However, Women's Studies
resources are also located throughout the entire collection
in the appropriate subject classifications: art, music,
history, literature, etc. Therefore, this volume count is
very low. The Government Documents Department holds
important resources for Women's Studies as well. Serials
titles number about 70. Current imprints are in very high

demand, so added copies are purchased as needed. The Women's Studies collection at UCSD grew with the dramatic rise in the interest in that area in the late sixties. Anita Schiller initiated retrospective acquisitions anticipating future research needs. However, collection development of research level historical materials is severely limited by what is actually in print.

II.   Programmatic Needs

Currently thirty-two UCSD faculty teach courses on women and gender. Each year about 35 courses on women's issues are taught at UCSD.

Many faculty have published books on women's topics in the past five years. The 1991-92 edition of Women and Gender: a Directory of UCSD Faculty and Graduate Students provides entries for 126 members of UCSD scholarly community studying women and gender issues. In Fall 1982, UCSD offered a Women's Studies Minor for the first time, increasing the visibility of the existing courses and the pressure on library resources in that area. In Fall 1989, a Women's Studies Program Director was appointed to plan for a Women's Studies major and a graduate level program. The Major was proposed in Spring 1991.

The Women's Studies collection meets the needs of most undergraduate students (NCIP 3). Graduate students and faculty, however, must rely on interlibrary loan to obtain much of the retrospective material related to their research. Some resources are available for purchase on microfilm; however, students and faculty prefer to use paper copy when it is available. UCSD has purchased several microform sets which are now listed in the UCSD Library publication American Women's History, a Pathfinder. Bibliographic access to larger microform sets which relate to women remains limited.

III.   Collection Guidelines

Since Women's Studies is a highly inter-disciplinary program, all subject bibliographers collect for their areas and meet the primary needs of their faculty and students. The Women's Studies bibliographer evaluates major interdisciplinary sets and serials and purchases the majority of the retrospective materials, including some in government documents.

The Central Library purchases most current U.S. imprints on Women's Studies, thus meeting most undergraduate needs. Retrospective collection development is limited to sources still in print, reprints and microform sets. Most materials are in English; however small French, German and Italian collections are being developed to meet graduate students needs. Most materials are monographs. The serials collection remains small. The library will not purchase most of the major microform sets currently available through interlibrary loan, though special efforts will be made to purchase more guides to these sets to provide easier access to their detailed contents and speed the interlibrary loan process. Rare books and journals of high cost are normally not collected.

IV.   Regional and National Sources

San Diego State University offers a large Women's Studies Program. It has a significant journal collection and a major monographic collection to support that program. UCLA, UC Berkeley and UC and UC Santa Barbara all have major Women's Studies collections, including expensive microform sets and archival materials.

SG:mh
9/89
michele\cmg\sg\women.col
rev. 1991

UNIVERSITY OF DELAWARE LIBRARY

WOMEN'S STUDIES COLLECTION DEVELOPMENT POLICY STATEMENT

Draft

January 1992

Purpose

The collection supports present and anticipated teaching and research in the field of Women's Studies and its subdisciplines. At present, the central focus of the program and chief interests of the faculty are encompassed in the following areas of teaching and research: the historical and contemporary lives and concerns of women, and the influence of gender on the human experience. In addition to being a unique field with its own philosophy, methodology, and resources, Women's Studies provides the impetus toward reexamining each of the traditional scholarly disciplines to identify and correct misinformation and unexamined assumptions about "women's place" in history.

The program offers a minor in Women's Studies and, through the Liberal Studies degree program, an individually designed major. In addition to the support for the Women's Studies Program, the collection, especially in view of its broad interdisciplinary nature, also serves as a resource for undergraduate and graduate students and faculty in other disciplines. Related colleges, departments, and programs covering subjects of interest to Women's Studies include: American Studies; Anthropology; Art History; Black American

Studies; Business Administration; Center for Science and Culture; Communication; Comparative Literature; Criminal Justice; Economics; Education; English; Foreign Languages and Literatures; History; Individual and Family Studies; Latin American Studies; Life and Health Sciences; Music; Nursing; Philosophy; Physical Education; Political Science; Psychology; Sociology; Textiles, Design and Consumer Economics; and Theatre.

Because Women's Studies is such a highly interdisciplinary collecting area, the selector for Women's Studies has close ties with selectors for other disciplines. The Women's Studies selector maintains close communication with selectors in the social sciences and humanities, especially in the following areas: English, History, Individual and Family Studies, History, Political Science, and Sociology.

Languages

The primary language of acquisition is English. Materials in French and Spanish are acquired selectively, and in the original only if no translation is available. Materials in other foreign languages are not normally acquired.

Chronological Guidelines

All historical periods are of interest; however, primary emphasis is on women in the nineteenth and twentieth centuries.

Geographical Guidelines

All geographic regions are of interest, although primary

emphasis is on women in the United States and Great Britain. Works about women in non-Western cultures are of special interest. For local history, materials on the mid-Atlantic region (i.e. Delaware, Maryland, New Jersey, Pennsylvania, and Virginia) are of particular interest.

Treatment of Subject

Theoretical works and published research on women or gender studies are of primary importance. Of particular interest are materials on the historical, political, social, and psychological aspects of the woman's experience. Also of primary interest are materials on feminist theory and methodology.

Autobiographies, biographies, published diaries and journals, and travel literature are of interest when their content illustrates the social and/or cultural context of women. Literary works (e.g. novels, poetry, anthologies, etc.) by women authors that address the condition of women are selectively acquired.

Popular publications, for example, self-help materials in the fields of psychology, business, and health care are collected on a highly selective basis.

Juvenile literature, and elementary and secondary level textbooks specifically addressing women's history are selectively acquired. Textbooks at the advanced level are acquired on a selective basis.

Types of Material

Monographs and serials published by university, trade and

small presses form the basis for acquisition. Materials published by small presses and independent publishers are actively acquired. Reference materials, including bibliographies, handbooks, dictionaries, and library and museum catalogs, are of primary interest.

Publications of U.S. government agencies (e.g. Bureau of the Census, Dept. of Education) are acquired either through the U.S. Federal Depository Program or other sources.

Publications of national and international organizations, societies, and congresses (e.g. National Organization for Women, National Women's Studies Association, International Labour Organisation, United Nations Commission on the Status of Women) are acquired on a selective basis.

Publications of college and university Women's Studies programs or departments and of related departments or programs are acquired on a selective basis. Theses and dissertations from other institutions are not normally collected.

Original manuscript and archival materials are not actively collected, although microform reproductions are acquired selectively.

Major sets and collections of material which significantly supplement existing resources are selectively acquired.

Date of Publication

Emphasis is on materials published within the past ten years. Retrospective materials are acquired when appropriate with no preference as to format, i.e. original, reprint, or microform.

<u>Related Subject Policy Statements</u>

Other relevant information related to Women's Studies will be found in the following policy statements:

American Studies: women and American life and culture

Anthropology: women in society, women's culture

Art History: images of women in art, women as artists

Black American Studies: African-American women, women in the Caribbean; race, class and gender

Business Administration: women in business

Communication: mass media and women, sex role in advertising

Comparative Literature: women in comparative literature, women authors, feminist literary criticism

Criminal Justice: female offenders, violence against women

Economics: women and development, women in the workforce

Education: women's education, women's roles in education

English: biographies and criticism of women authors, women in literature, feminist literary criticism

Ethnic Studies: ethnic and minority women in the United States; gender and ethnicity

Foreign Language and Literature: biographies and criticism of women authors, women in romance literature, feminist literary criticism

History: history of women, historical biographies of women

Individual and Family Studies: family life, domestic relations, life span development of women

Latin American Studies: women in Latin America, Latin American women writers

Music: women in music

Life and Health Sciences: women's health issues, women as
    health care providers

Nursing: women's health issues, women as health care providers

Philosophy: philosophy of women and of feminism, women
    philosophers, feminist ethics

Physical Education: women in sports and physical education

Political Science: women in politics, women in political
    movements

Psychology: sex-role socialization, psychology of women,
    psychology of men

Science and Culture: women and science, women's health issues

Sociology: gender relations; social problems affecting women;
    groups and classes of women; race, class, and gender.

Textiles, Design and Consumer Economics: women's apparel
    industry, women and clothing

Theatre: feminist theater, women in theater

<u>Levels of Collecting Intensity by Subject Subdivision</u>

	<u>Collecting Level</u>
Anthropology	
Cross-cultural studies of women	B
Women in society	B
Women's culture	B
Arts and Music	
Feminist film theory	B
Feminist theater	B

Image of women in the performing arts   B

Women and music   B

Women artists   B

Women performing artists   B

Women's art   B

Business and Economics

Economics of women's labor   B

Women and development   B

Women in labor unions   B

Women in the workforce   B

Communications, Language, and Linguistics

Sex role in the mass media   B

Women in the mass media industry   B

Women's communication style   B

Education

Feminist pedagogy   B

History of women's education   B

Women's roles in education   B

Women's Studies as a discipline   B

Ethnic Studies

Ethnic and minority women   B

Gender and ethnicity   B

Feminist Theory   B

History

Women's history, United States, eighteenth-century

     to the present   B

Women's history, United States, pre-eighteenth

century	C
Women's history, Great Britain, eighteenth century	
to the present	B
Women's history, Great Britain, pre-eighteenth century	C
Women's history, other countries, all periods	C

Regional and local history

Mid-atlantic region, United States	B
Other regions in the United States	C
Other countries	C

Life and Health Sciences

Anatomy and physiology of women	B
Reproduction and childbirth	B
Women as health care providers	B
Women's health issues	B

Literature and Biography

Autobiography and Biography	C
Feminist literary criticism	B
Lesbian literature	C
Literary works by women	B
Travel literature by women	C
Women in literature	B

Men's Studies	B

Political Science, Criminial Justice, and Legal Studies

Crimes against women	B
Female offenders	B
Women and legal reform	B
Women in criminal justice administration	B

Women in politics	B
Women in political movements	B
Women in the legal profession	B

Psychology

Interpersonal relations	B
Psychology of women	B
Psychopathology and women	B
Sex-role socialization	B
Women and psychoanalytic theory	B
Women in the psychology profession	B

Religion and Philosophy

Feminist ethics	B
Feminist theology	C
Women and spiritualism (e.g. goddess worship, witchcraft, etc.)	C
Women in organized religions	C
Women in the Bible	C

Science and Technology

Scientific theories on gender	B
Technology and women	B
Women in science and technology	B

Sociology

Gender relations	B
Groups and classes of women (e.g. ethnic women, housewives, lesbians, prostitutes, etc.)	B
Race, class, and gender studies	B
Social problems affecting women	B

Women and the family   B

Sports and Physical Education

    Role of women in sports   B

    Women and physical education   B

    Women athletes   B

Women's Rights Movement   B

UNIVERSITY OF ILLINOIS AT URBANA-CHAMPAIGN
WOMEN'S STUDIES/WOMEN IN INTERNATIONAL DEVELOPMENT
Beth Stafford; November 1985
Revised: January 1990

I. DESCRIPTION

A. Purpose: The collection supports the work of the Women's Studies
Program, which is committed to promote and administer instruction and advanced
research on women, within and across disciplines, including work on the roles,
status and history of women; women in literature and the arts; public policy
issues relating to women; international studies and women, and research and
teaching that involve the sexuality and physiology of women. A certificate in
Women's Studies is administered by the Women's Studies Program, and
undergraduates may major in Women's Studies through the Individual Plans of
Study program. Faculty interested in Women's Studies come from several
schools and colleges within the university, including Education, Agriculture,
Humanities, Social Sciences, and Medicine.

B. History of Collection: Women's Studies is a young multidisciplinary
field that began in 1969, when the first college course in Women's Studies was
offered in this country. On this campus, the first Women's Studies course was
offered in 1970. Although a sizeable body of library materials relevant to
Women's Studies has been acquired in the course of building the outstanding
library collection on this campus, no systematic attempts were made to collect
materials in the field until 1974. At that time, a library faculty member
started acquiring only monographs on general state funds. A separate Women's
Studies fund for monographs was established in 1978. Coinciding with the
establishment of the Office of Women's Studies, a full-time Women's Studies
Bibliographer position was established in the fall of 1979, and funds were
allocated for the acquisition of both serials and monographs.

C. Estimate of Holdings: Because materials in a variety of disciplines
are spread throughout the library system, the number of monographs relevant to
women's studies is difficult to estimate. Serial titles number at least 622.

D. State, Regional and National Importance: Most comprehensive single
collection in Women's Studies in the state and region. In terms of published
materials the collection in the area of women in the United States, is
probably second only to Harvard's Schlesinger Library on the History of Women
in America, housed at Radcliffe College. In terms of overall
comprehensiveness, especially in international coverage, it probably ranks the
same in importance as the Library as a whole. Primary source materials are
found mainly in the extensive Marital Rape Collection, the Illinois Historical
Survey, and University Archives. The Library has recently acquired the Marital
Rape Collection, a unique collection of national importance in Women's
Studies.

E. Unit Responsible for Collection: Office of the Women's Studies/Women
in International Development Librarian.

----
*The title is now Women's Studies/Women in International Development
Librarian.

F. Location of Materials: The collection is scattered throughout most of the library system, with approximately one third of it in the Bookstacks.

G. Citation of Works Describing the Collection: None.

II. GENERAL COLLECTION GUIDELINES

A. Languages: Standard statement.

B. Chronological Guidelines: No restrictions.

C. Geographic Guidelines: Worldwide scope.

D. Treatment of Subject: Standard statement. Materials with primary focus on females of all age groups in all historical periods and cultures or on gender-related phenomena. Materials about issues of special concern to women. Feminist studies, ie., works that are self-identified as feminist or are identified by critics as feminist, or which present a feminist perspective or are about feminism, are of special concern. Due to the multidisciplinary nature of Women's Studies, there are overlaps in collecting responsibilities with those of other Library selectors, especially within the social science, humanities, and area studies libraries and collections. Women's Studies collects a limited amount of children's and young adult literature and school curricular materials.

E. Types of Materials: Standard statement.

F. Date of Publication: Standard statement.

G. Place of Publication: No restrictions.

III. COLLECTION RESPONSIBILITY BY SUBJECT SUBDIVISIONS WITH QUALIFICATIONS, LEVELS OF COLLECTING INTENSITY, AND ASSIGNMENTS

SUBJECT	ES	CL	DL	ASSIGNMENTS
Economics and Business	3	3	3	COMMERCE/ women's studies
Credit (finance) and women	3	3	3	WOMEN'S STUDIES
Poverty and women	3	3	4	WOMEN'S STUDIES
Unpaid work of women	3	3	3	WOMEN'S STUDIES
Family economics	3	3	3	women's studies
Economic development planning	3	3	3	women's studies
Int'l economic development planning	3	3	3	women's studies
Women & economic theory	3	3	3	WOMEN'S STUDIES
Occupational sex/race segregation	3	3	3	women's studies
Labor and Industrial Relations	3	3	3	LABOR/ women's studies
Labor unions and women	3	3	3	WOMEN'S STUDIES
Labor markets and women	3	3	3	WOMEN'S STUDIES
Labor law - discrimination	3	3	3	women's studies
Labor movements and women	3	3	3	WOMEN'S STUDIES

SUBJECT	ES	CL	DL	ASSIGNMENTS
Geography and women	1	2	3	WOMEN'S STUDIES
Women and planning	1	2	3	WOMEN'S STUDIES
Women in International Development	3	3	4	WOMEN'S STUDIES/ agriculture
Economic devel. planning & women	3	3	4	WOMEN'S STUDIES/ agriculture
Technology and women	3	3	4	WOMEN'S STUDIES/ agriculture
Water supplies and women	3	3	4	WOMEN'S STUDIES
Energy sources and women	3	3	4	WOMEN'S STUDIES
History and women	3	3	3	women's studies
Women's history, ancient to present	3	3	3	women's studies
Women's history, global	3	3	3	women's studies
Biographies and diaries of women	3	3	3	women's studies
Regional women's history	3	3	4	women's studies
Illinois women's history	3	3	4	women's studies
Reference works (Women's Studies)	3	3	4	WOMEN'S STUDIES
Education and women	2	3	4	EDUCATION/ women's studies
Sexism in the curriculum	2	3	4	WOMEN'S STUDIES
Sexism in children's and young adults' literature	2	3	4	WOMEN'S STUDIES
Education and females	2	3	4	EDUCATION/ women's studies
Sexism in the classroom	2	3	4	WOMEN'S STUDIES
Instructional materials and gender	2	3	4	WOMEN'S STUDIES
Sports and women	2	3	3	women's studies
Language/communication and women	3	3	4	WOMEN'S STUDIES
Sexism in language	3	3	4	WOMEN'S STUDIES
Philosophy of language and women	3	3	4	WOMEN'S STUDIES
Language and gender	3	3	4	WOMEN'S STUDIES
Media criticism	3	3	4	women's studies
Women's languages	3	3	4	WOMEN'S STUDIES
Law and women	3	3	3	women's studies
Legal status of females	3	3	3	women's studies
Rights of lesbian mothers	3	3	3	WOMEN'S STUDIES
Battered women	3	3	3	women's studies
Marital rape	3	4	4	WOMEN'S STUDIES
Psychology and women	3	3	3	women's studies
Sex roles	3	3	3	women's studies
Sexual harrassment	3	3	4	WOMEN'S STUDIES
Sexuality	3	3	3	women's studies
Humor and gender	3	3	3	women's studies
Achievement motivation in females	3	3	3	WOMEN'S STUDIES

SUBJECT	ES	CL	DL	ASSIGNMENTS
Non-verbal interpersonal communication and gender	3	3	4	women's studies
Violence against girls and women	3	3	3	women's studies
Feminist humor	3	3	3	WOMEN'S STUDIES
Political science and women	3	3	4	POLITICAL SCIENCE/ women's studies
Politics and women	3	3	4	women's studies
Public policy and females	3	3	4	WOMEN'S STUDIES
Sexual politics	3	3	4	WOMEN'S STUDIES
Peace (disarmament) movements and women	3	3	4	WOMEN'S STUDIES
The military and women	3	3	4	WOMEN'S STUDIES
Women in social & political movements	3	3	4	WOMEN'S STUDIES
National liberation movements and women/females	2	3	4	WOMEN'S STUDIES
Women's rights	3	3	4	WOMEN'S STUDIES
International women's movements	2	3	4	WOMEN'S STUDIES
Political participation of women	3	3	4	WOMEN'S STUDIES
Civil rights and sexual preference	3	3	4	women's studies
Gender politics	3	3	4	WOMEN'S STUDIES
Anthropology and sociology and women	3	3	3	ANTHROPOLOGY/ SOCIOLOGY/ women's studies
Sex roles	3	3	3	women's studies
Matriarchal societies & traditions	3	3	4	WOMEN'S STUDIES
Dual career couples	3	3	3	women's studies
Lesbian studies	3	3	3	WOMEN'S STUDIES
Age and women	3	3	3	WOMEN'S STUDIES
Ethnic women (globally)	3	3	3	WOMEN'S STUDIES
Migration and women	3	3	3	WOMEN'S STUDIES
Race and gender	3	3	3	WOMEN'S STUDIES
Class and gender	3	3	3	WOMEN'S STUDIES
Sexuality	3	3	3	women's studies
Sexuality and gender	3	3	3	WOMEN'S STUDIES
Gender studies	3	3	3	WOMEN'S STUDIES
Battered women	3	3	3	WOMEN'S STUDIES
Violence against girls and women	3	3	3	WOMEN'S STUDIES
Disabled women	3	3	3	WOMEN'S STUDIES
Patriarchy	3	3	4	WOMEN'S STUDIES
Literature and women	3	3	4	ENGLISH,etc/ women's studies
Women's literature	3	3	4	women's studies
Lesbian literature	3	3	4	WOMEN'S STUDIES
Feminist criticism	3	3	4	WOMEN'S STUDIES
Feminist literature (all languages)	3	3	4	WOMEN'S STUDIES
Fine arts and women	3	3	3	women's studies
Feminist aesthetic	3	3	3	WOMEN'S STUDIES
Feminist criticism	3	3	3	WOMEN'S STUDIES
Art criticism	3	3	3	women's studies

SUBJECT	ES	CL	DL	ASSIGNMENTS
Art history	3	3	3	women's studies
Performing Arts and Women	3	3	3	MUSIC/theatre/ women's studies
Music, Women's	3	3	3	WOMEN'S STUDIES
Feminist criticism	3	3	3	WOMEN'S STUDIES
Theatre, Women's	3	3	3	WOMEN'S STUDIES
Religion (s) and women	2	3	3	WOMEN'S STUDIES
Feminist theology	3	3	3	WOMEN'S STUDIES
Philosophy	3	3	3	women's studies
Feminist theory	3	3	3	WOMEN'S STUDIES
Science, technology and women	3	3	3	WOMEN'S STUDIES/ agriculture
Science and women	3	3	3	WOMEN'S STUDIES
Technology and women	3	3	3	WOMEN'S STUDIES/ agriculture
Agriculture and women	3	3	3	AGRICULTURE/ women's studies
Health and women	2	3	3	WOMEN'S STUDIES
Women's health movement	2	3	3	WOMEN'S STUDIES
Community services	2	3	3	WOMEN'S STUDIES
Personal health	2	3	3	WOMEN'S STUDIES
Drug-related problems and women	2	3	3	WOMEN'S STUDIES
Emotional/mental health and women	2	3	4	WOMEN'S STUDIES

SUBJECT	ES	CL	DL	ASSIGNMENTS

GENERAL INTRODUCTION

This collection development statement is a written guide to the University Library's effort to support the instructional and research activities being undertaken at the University of Illinois at Urbana-Champaign. The most immediate use of the statement is for the Library faculty to identify as clearly as possible the areas of collecting responsibilities among the numerous library units which provide informational services and library materials to a comprehensive university, offering the Ph.D. degree in over 90 subjects and supporting numerous independent research facilities as well as a full range of undergraduate, Master's, and professional programs. The policy statement is also intended to be a guide to the teaching faculty and university administrators to facilitate their understanding of the collections and the vast network of collection development activities taking place in the third largest academic library in the country, which in 1986 purchased its seven millionth volume. Collection policies for academic libraries are first and foremost directed to the institution which they serve. But this document should also be useful to other libraries which seek to comprehend this library's collection profile and policies in order to develop resource sharing and cooperative collection development agreements.

This is not the Library's first attempt at providing a guide to its collection policies. The Library first adopted an Acquisition Policy Statement in 1959. That statement was revised five times by 1976. Because of the rapid growth of collections, as well as new developments in the field of collection development, the Acquisition Policy Statement was found to be inadequate. A completely new format and guidelines were devised in 1983 in order to produce a more useful document for present needs.

All units under the jurisdiction of the University of Illinois at Urbana-Champaign Library fall within the purview of this policy statement. These units include over 40 departmental libraries, area studies libraries and special bibliographic units, and special collections. There are a number of other libraries and reading rooms on the Urbana-Champaign campus, such as the Geological Survey and Water Survey Libraries, the Computer Science Department Library, the Residence Hall Library, and the Health Science Library. These are not part of the University Library system; nor do they affect the collection policies of the Library, with the exception of the latter library. While administered by the University of Illinois at Chicago Library, the Health Sciences Library is on the Urbana-Champaign campus and its materials are easily accessible. For these reasons, the University of Illinois at Urbana-Champaign Library does not collect materials in clinical medicine, except material needed for Veterinary Medicine.

This document is a compilation of individual collection development statements prepared and revised by more than 50 selectors from 1983 through 1989. These statements for the most part describe the collection development activities connected to a particular subject fund and the title of each statement is the name of such a fund. In addition, there are statements which describe collection development activities related to collections for which no specific funds are required for the acquisition of materials, such as the Documents Library and the University Archives, or collections which use a variety of funds for collection building because of their general nature, such as the Rare Book and Special Collections Library and the Media Center. Thus, each statement represents the author's understanding of the scope of the collection responsibility related to the specific fund or collection. It will be noted, however, that no selector controls all aspects of a particular subject area. In practically every field, cooperation and coordination of collection building with other selectors are required.

Certain collecting policies encourage this vision of the Library and actually facilitate the practice of cooperation and coordination of selection activities. First of all, there is the administrative aspect of collection development carried out by the Office of the Director of Collection Development and Special Collections, the Collection Development Committee, and Special Collections Administration which provide lines of communications and a structure to these activities. Secondly, there are funding and acquisition arrangements which are centrally administered and are beneficial to individual libraries and to the collection as a whole.

Some of these funds finance approval plans and blanket orders, which are agreements with selected vendors to supply current publications as soon as they are published according to specified guidelines. The three general acquisitions plans of this type are: 1.) the University Press Blanket Order, which includes over 100 U.S., Canadian, and British University presses in all subjects except clinical medicine and excluding lower level text books and reprints; 2.) the Publisher-Based Approval Plan, which includes approximately 80 American and British commercial publishers with the same exclusions described above; and 3.) the European Blanket Order for current publications from Austria, East Germany, West Germany, Switzerland, France, Italy, and Spain based on a broad subject profile of 35 categories in the humanities (excluding music, art, and architecture), and the social sciences. (For fuller description of these programs, see the University of Illinois Library's Policy and Procedures Manual, 425/4.)

Mention must also be made of the area studies programs and how they benefit the collection as a whole. The nature of the area studies is that they are both general in subject coverage and specialized in terms of language and geographical area. These units are established to facilitate the acquisition and processing of materials from areas of the world which require special handling and language expertise. As a general rule, works in the humanities and social sciences published in Eastern Europe, the Soviet Union, East Asia (China, Japan, Korea), South and West Asia (Indian Subcontinent and the Middle East), Sub-Saharan Africa and Latin America and with a subject focus on these areas are within the collecting responsibilities of the area studies. Responsibilities for works about these areas published in English and other languages outside these areas vary, as indicated in individual statements.

FORMAT AND GUIDE TO STATEMENTS

To provide editorial control and standardized and comparable information, all authors of the statements were required to follow the same outline. Each statement is divided into three sections: I. Description, II. General Collection Guidelines, and III. Collection Responsibility.

Section I, Description, is devoted to a description of a particular collection and consists of seven parts: A. <u>Purpose</u>, which describes the general purpose of the collection and identifies specific teaching and research programs using the collection most intensively; B. <u>History of Collection</u>, which points out significant events in the history of the collection as well as recognizing teaching faculty members and other benefactors who had influential roles in the development of the collection; C. <u>Estimate of Holdings</u>, which in most cases is a statement of holdings in a particular subject area throughout the Library system, or in a few cases, such as the Rare Book and Special Collections Library and the Law Library, the holdings statement represents only the materials in those discrete libraries; D. <u>State, Regional and National Importance</u>, which assesses the relative importance of the collection and enumerates particular strengths and special collections which make the collection especially significant; E. <u>Unit Responsible for Collecting</u>, which identifies the departmental library or bibliographic unit with primary responsibility for selection; F. <u>Location of Materials</u>, which specifies where relevant holdings are housed throughout the library system in various departmental libraries and the Bookstacks (a term used throughout this document to refer to the general bookstacks in the main library building); and G. <u>Citations of Works Describing the Collection</u>, which lists both published and unpublished works describing various aspects of the collection. Because of numerous citations to Robert B. Downs, Editor, <u>Guide to Illinois Library Resources</u> (Chicago: American Library Association, 1974) and Jean A. Major, Compiler, <u>Collections Acquired by the University of Illinois Library at Urbana-Champaign, 1897-1974</u> (University of Illinois Library and Graduate School of Library Science, 1974), citations for these works have been abbreviated to "Downs" and "Major" respectively.

Section II, General Collection Guidelines, describes current collection policies which guide the selection of materials related to a particular fund or collection. There are seven categories of collection guidelines: A. <u>Languages</u>, B. <u>Chronological Guidelines</u>, C. <u>Geographical Guidelines</u>, D. <u>Treatment of Subject</u>, E. <u>Types of Materials</u>, F. <u>Date of Publication</u>, and G. <u>Place of Publication</u>. The "languages" section refers to the languages in which the works are published. "Chronological" and "geographical guidelines" refer to the <u>subject content</u> of the material rather than to date or place of publication. Certain fields have specific chronological or geographical interests or emphases; others do not.

The "treatment of subject" defines two areas, the level of treatment, i.e., popular or scholarly, and the intellectual parameters of a subject or collection from the point of view of collecting responsibilities. The latter part in many cases will specify how various selectors may overlap in the coverage of a general subject matter by differentiating the kinds of intellectual treatments which make a subject relevant to the collecting interests of a variety of libraries.

"Types of materials" refers to the physical and bibliographic format of the works. "Date of publication" relates to the collecting of current and retrospective materials and "place of publication" to the origin of the work. Collecting policies or the patterns of publication in a given field may emphasize or actually restrict the countries from which publications are purchased.

Standard Statements

Certain guidelines are common to many fields of collecting and are described in the standard statements below. When the guidelines of individual collection development statements are represented by these standard statements, a reference is made to the appropriate standard statement. Necessary exceptions and deviations from these standard statements will be fully explained in the individual collection development statements. There are no standard statements for chronological guidelines, geographical guidelines, and place of publication. The standard statements for the remaining collection guidelines are as follows:

A. Languages: English is the dominant language of the collection. Materials in Western European languages are also collected in varying degrees of intensity. Materials in Slavic and Eastern European languages and materials in Asian and Middle Eastern languages are collected only in cooperation with the Slavic and Eastern European Library and the Asian Library respectively.

D. Treatment of Subject: Emphasis is on scholarly treatment rather than popularization, textbooks, and children's literature. The Undergraduate Library normally collects more popular treatments and the Education and Social Sciences Library collects children's literature for its School Collection.

E. Types of Materials: Appropriate primary and secondary works, and bibliographic, and reference materials are acquired. Ordinarily, dissertations, theses and translations are selectively collected. Hard copy is normally preferred to microforms except when the original formats are unavailable or prohibitively expensive, or for reasons of usage, storage or conservation/preservation, in which case microforms may be preferable. Audio-visual materials are normally collected selectively.

F. Date of Publication: Current materials are emphasized, but retrospective works are acquired on a selective basis. New and revised editions of important works are purchased when new explanatory or primary material is introduced.

Section III, Collection Responsibility by Subject Subdivision with Qualifications, Levels of Collecting Intensity, and Assignments, consists of three parts. The first part, Subjects, is a column listing the subject subdivisions within the scope of the fund or collection being described. The subject headings are not derived from a single standardized list such as Library of Congress or Dewey classification headings. This is because no single list of headings was found to be adequate for all fields of knowledge. The subject headings in each statement represent what the authors believe are the terms most often used or are most useful for describing the collection. The subjects from each statement are listed alphabetically in the subject index. The middle columns refer to the level of strength and collecting intensity for each subject category. The collecting levels, 1-5, are based on the "collection intensity indicators" used in the Research Libraries Group's conspectus but are modified for local use. In most statements, the level of holdings and collecting intensity for a particular subject reflect the Library system-wide, that is, the combined figures for various departmental libraries and the Bookstacks. In some cases, such as the statements for the Asian

Library, the Law Library, and the Rare Book and Special Collections Library, i.e., units which are more self-contained, the figures are for those units only. The five levels of collecting intensity are defined as follows:

Collecting Levels

1. General: A selective collection serving to introduce and define the subject and to indicate the varieties of information which are available elsewhere. It shall include some textbooks, dictionaries, encyclopedias, selected editions of important works of major authors, historical surveys, biographies, bibliographies and several periodicals for keeping in touch with current scholarship in the field.

2. Undergraduate Instruction: A good working collection designed to meet all instructional needs. It shall include a wide range of basic works, complete collections of the works of more important figures, both authors and critics, selections from the works of secondary writers, yearbooks, handbooks, a wide range of representative journals, and the fundamental bibliographical apparatus pertaining to the subject.

3. Research and Graduate Study: A collection supporting graduate instruction and continuing research or likely future research at the dissertation level. It shall include the major published source materials required for dissertation and independent research, all important reference works, and a wide selection of specialized monographs and other secondary literature as well as an extensive collection of journals. Allows for selective programs of retrospective purchasing.

4. Comprehensive Research: A comprehensive collection to support advanced research. It shall include all important or useful works, original editions of the classics in the field, and an extensive assemblage of critical and biographical works, contemporary pamphlets, published documents, and the fullest possible list of journal sets and bibliographical tools. Allows for extensive programs of retrospective purchasing and searching for lacunae.

5. Exhaustive Research: A collection including as far as possible all publications such as manuscripts, archives, and ephemera. Such collecting will be undertaken only in restricted areas, such as materials by a single literary or historical person. The only areas in which the Library collects exhaustively are: Abraham Lincoln, W. S. Merwin, Marcel Proust, Carl Sandburg, William Shakespeare, and H.G. Wells.

These numbers are used to indicate for each subject subdivision the CS or "current strength" of the collection, the CL or 'current level" of collecting intensity, and DL or "desired level" of collecting to support new developments in teaching and research programs, and other anticipated need.

The last part of Section III is the Assignments column which lists the funds that are assigned for purchasing material in a given subject category. The name of the fund with the primary assignment of responsibility is indicated in capital letters, and those with secondary responsibility are noted in small letters. In a few cases, more than one fund may have equal and primary responsibilities. This situation stems from heavy demand for materials and reveals areas of necessary cooperation and duplication.

* * *

The compilation and editing of this policy statement were complex and time-consuming tasks, especially because of the multifaceted nature and size of the University of Illinois Library at Urbana-Champaign. To a large degree, however, it is the process itself of creating this policy statement that is the most important aspect of assembling this document. This process involves the individual librarian's assessment of the collections for which he/she is responsible; the analysis of current and possible future demands placed on these resources; and the articulation of this information to colleagues in verbal and written form. These activities sharpen a selector's awareness of the collection development process as well as his/her ability to select materials wisely.

The major responsibility for working with the individual librarians who composed these statements fell upon the former Assistant to the Director of Library Collections, Mr. Robert Sewell, who has written this general introduction. Additional editing and revision was provided by his successor, in the same position, Ms. Ann Leighton. To them both, and especially to the selectors who contributed to this statement, I wish to express the Library's gratitude for this excellent document which will guide our efforts in collection development for many years to come.

Carl W. Deal
Director of Collection Development
and Special Collections

[From: Collection Development Policy for the University of Kansas Libraries. 2nd ed. Lawrence:University of Kansas Libraries. In press, 1992.]

Draft 1/92

WOMEN'S STUDIES

Principal Selector: Mary M. Rosenbloom
Principal Location: Watson Library

I. Definition

A. Subject

The 1990-91 brochure produced by the Women's Studies Program defines the KU program as "an interdisciplinary program of courses that places emphasis on women, their history, an understanding of their contemporary status, and a consideration of their future possibilities." The Dictionary of Feminist Theory notes that the academic discipline "Woman's Studies" is not divorced from political and social movements, but has been described as the intellectual and research arm of the women's movement. And indeed the KU brochure goes on to state, "Women's Studies focuses on women's experiences in part because they have been largely ignored or undervalued in other areas of the curriculum."

B. User Population

The primary users of the women's studies collection are difficult to identify since any number of faculty and graduate students throughout the university may be working on inter-disciplinary topics related to women's studies. The core user group might be considered the Women' Studies Advisory Board which has 30 members. The Women's Studies Program Newsletter is mailed to over 150 people campuswide who have declared interests in women's studies. Departments which have shown sustained commitment to the Women's Studies Program include English, History, American Studies, Sociology, Religious Studies, Communications and Psychology.

The Program does not currently offer a graduate program although it is projected that approximately 45 graduate students are currently working on theses or dissertations relating to women. The Program is seriously considering offering some sort of recognition (such as a certificate) to graduate students who work in areas of interest to women's studies. In spring 1990 the Program had 17 declared majors, and nearly 650 students enrolled in women's studies courses or courses cross-listed with the Women's Studies Program.

C. Collection Characteristics

The strength of the women's studies collection lies in the library's long-time commitment to purchasing in this area. Books on women and the status of women were singled out for purchase well before women's studies as an academic discipline became common. The Gerritsen Collection on the History of Women was purchased in the 1950s from the John Crerar Library, and Richard S. Howey, bibliographer for social history from 1930-1989, counted books about women as a particular interest. In response to the formation of a Women's Studies Program on the KU campus, a bibliographer was given responsibility for the collection in 1974. In this second wave of interest, attention has been paid both to the scholarly research produced by academics, and the popular and political literature which was spawned by the women's movement.

When checking bibliographies of women's studies materials, it is not unusual to find that KU owns every title on the list. Our collection is strongest from the 1970s onward, but we have excellent 19th-century holdings on U.S. women. Because the faculty most active in the Women's Studies Program have come from the disciplines of history and literature, the collection is strongest in those areas, and has focused on American women's experience. More recently attention has been given to violence towards women, sociology of women, feminist philosophy, ethnic women and women in developing countries.

Approximately 110 serial titles are purchased with women's studies funds, and other titles of interest to women's studies are purchased through history (Journal of Women's History), sociology, and other funds. The titles range from scholarly journals such as Signs, and Women's Studies International, to literary magazines such as Sinister Wisdom, to radical magazines such as Trouble and Strife.

The collection includes several major microform sets, including The Gerritsen Collection, History of Women, Papers of the Women's Trade Union League, National Women's Party Papers and others.

II. Collection Guidelines

A. Parameters

English language materials predominate, although materials in French (from France, Canada and the Caribbean) and German are purchased on a regular basis. Some materials in Spanish on Hispanic women in America are purchased, although a separate fund is available for Hispanic materials. Few other foreign language materials are purchased, although materials in English from throughout the world are collected. Emphasis is placed on purchasing current publications, although historical microform sets and some out-of-print titles are purchased.

B. Types of Media

Books and serials, either in hard copy or microform, are the only types of media currently purchased for the women's studies collection.

C. Collecting Priorities

--Scholarly books and periodicals written from a feminist perspective in all disciplines, but especially in history, language and literature, psychology and sociology.

--Records of women's experience written by the women themselves, especially if these records are consciously feminist: autobiography, diaries, oral history and literature.

--Materials published by groups directly involved in the women's movement.

--Reference materials which provide access to the literature and facts concerning the status of women.

--Lesbian literature because of its often radical perspective on women's lives.

--Writings of and about non-white and non-U.S. women's experience are also purchased widely.

--Primary resources for research.

--Out-of-print literature by women.

III. Future Directions

Interdisciplinary programs at KU have just been reviewed and the Women's Studies Program received extremely high marks. It is a vital program on campus. In recent years feminist scholars have been appointed in several departments, and a new half-time position in women and race has been added to the Women's Studies Program. This position has been filled by a dynamic and multi-talented African scholar who will bring a new perspective to the Program.

Catherine Stimpson, founder of the journal <u>Signs</u> and president of the Modern Language Association, spoke at the annual ALA conference in Chicago. She outlined three areas of development in the field of women's studies: women in developing countries, the history of women's studies, and women and religion.

As the study of women's experience and consciousness takes a leading role in academia, writing and publishing in this area have flourished. Women's studies have come into the mainstream and the current proliferation of reference works (defining, categorizing and controlling the trends and research) attests to this fact. Thus the focus of collecting women's studies library materials has changed from building to broadening the scope of the collection and expanding the primary resources.

IV. Selection Process

A. Method of Receipt
Excellent coverage of U.S. and British university presses and the larger commercial publishers is provided by the approval plans.
Canadian and Australian materials are also received in this manner, although coverage is more selective. Most of the orders I place are for small press, foreign, literary and non-scholarly materials.

B. Selection Tools
Bibliographies of current women's studies publications are produced by the University of Wisconsin, Women's Studies Bibliographer at Large. I also rely heavily on

<u>Feminist Bookstore News</u>, which announces forthcoming books from feminist and lesbian small presses. <u>Review of Women's Books</u> is also helpful, although most orders are placed before book reviews are published. For German and French materials I rely on the selection forms sent by vendors. In instances where I have some question as to the worthiness of an item I will seek advice from the book chair of the Women's Studies Advisory Board.

C. User Input
Suggestions for purchase are occasionally received from library users and faculty, and when monies are available and the item is suitable for the collection, the item is purchased.

V. System Coordination and Resource Sharing

Because of the interdisciplinary nature of women's studies, coordination with other bibliographers is important. For women and health I am in contact with the science library; for materials on Hispanic women I am in contact with the SPLAT bibliographer, etc. I have the most interaction with the general history, American history, American and English literature, and sociology bibliographers. In my interactions with these and other bibliographers I do not simply agree to buy any item about women. If the book has a conscious feminist or radical slant, or deals with women's political movements or the status or condition of women, I will buy it without question. However, if the item is merely a conventional history or study which covers women, I leave it to the specific subject bibliographer.

The Kansas Collection and the Special Collections Department both have interests in collecting women's materials. The Kansas Collection includes archives of women's organizations, manuscript diaries and the like.

The Emily Taylor Resource Center maintains a collection of books and serials to aid women in making life decisions.

VI. List of Main LC Classes Represented

HQ

UNIVERSITY OF PITTSBURGH

ACQUISITIONS POLICY - WOMEN'S STUDIES

Bibliographer: Adelaide Sukiennik   Library: Hillman

(1) General Purpose

The women's studies collection supports coursework offered by the Women's Studies Program of the Faculty of Arts and Sciences. It also supports the research and teaching needs of faculty in all parts of the University who deal with women's issues and the research needs of students in all parts of the University who write papers, masters theses, or doctoral dissertations pertaining to women.

(2) Languages

Most books acquired are written in English. Some foreign language material, especially in French and German, is purchased occasionally.

(3) Geographical Areas

Geographical treatment is worldwide, but the majority of books purchased pertain to women in the United States, Canada, and Great Britain because more books are published encompassing these areas.

Intensity of collecting is as follows:

United States	4	Europe	2
Great Britain	3	Latin America	2
Canada	3	Africa	2
Australia	2	Asia	2

(4) Chronological Limitations

The emphasis in acquisitions is on current imprints. Retrospective buying, including the purchase of reprints and microfilm sets, is done, according to curricular and research needs, and also according to the importance of the material for filling in gaps in the history of women and women's movements.

(5) Types of Materials Collected

Books and journals, both in print format and microform, are collected. Selected publications of small feminist presses are purchased, some for the main collection and some for Special Collections. A few introductory texts and dissertations are purchased very selectively, according to special needs.

(6) Types of Materials Excluded

Manuscripts, computerized data, and audiovisual materials are excluded. In general, most introductory tests and dissertations are also excluded, unless they fulfill a unique purpose and provide material otherwise unavailable.

(7) Subjects and Collecting Levels

Women's Studies is interdisciplinary, and books on the subject fall into all classification areas. These disparate areas - women in science, in mathematics, in medicine, in law, in politics, in art, in religion, for example - are all in demand by the user population described above, and collecting is done at Level 3, Beginning Research Level. If funds were available, Level 2 would be preferable.

In the classification area HQ1101-2030, Women, Feminism, Women's clubs, which is the heart of the women's studies collection, every effort is made to collect at the intensity of Level 2, Comprehensive Research. To this end, primary sources in reprint and microform are selected to provide material to augment the collection of current imprints.

July 1988

UNIVERSITY OF SOUTHERN CALIFORNIA LIBRARY
COLLECTION POLICY STATEMENT

Study of Women and Men in Society

* * *

I. ACADEMIC BACKGROUND INFORMATION

A. Programmatic Support for: [primary academic school, department]
Department of Study of Women and Men in Society

B. Major Instruction Emphases: [of the academic unit]
Literature (in general)
Anthropology
Sociology
Communications
Culture studies
Religion
Philosophy
History
Politics
Economics
Sports

C. Special Areas of Research Focus: [among the unit's faculty]
Women writers (emphasis on Western cultures)
Gender roles in society (cross cultural)
Gender defined communication (cross cultural)
Family studies (cross cultural)
Gender roles in economics/politics/public life
Feminist theory and philosophy
Gender psychology

D. Areas Specifically not of Interest: [to the academic unit]
Science, biology, technology, medicine

E. Degree programs in:
B.A., Study of Women and Men in Society
Minor, Study of Women and Men in Society
Graduate Certificate Program, Study of Women and Men in Society.

F. Collateral Academic Interest in: [other schools, departments]

Political Science	Anthropology	Communications
Classics	Law	Literature
Sociology	History	Journalism
Communications	Economics	Fine Arts/Art History
Gerontology	Religion	Cinema
Physical Education	Management	Economics
Psychology	Philosophy	

* * *

II. COLLECTION SCOPE

A. Languages:
__P__English ____Arabic ____Chinese ____Danish ____Dutch __S__French
__S__German ____Greek __S__Italian ____Japanese ____Korean ____Latin
____Norwegian ____Polish ____Portugues __S__Russian __S__Spanish ____Swedish
____No Lang. Limitations

B. Chronological Period:
__X___No Chronological Limitations
____Current Interests Only
_____Other:_____

C. Geographical Areas:
____U.S.____Canada____Western Europe____Eastern Europe ____Soviet Union
____Middle East____Latin America ____Africa____East Asia ____Southeast Asia
____Other Asia ____Australasia____Pacific Islands__X___No Geographical Limitations

D. Treatment of Subject:
_P___Scholarly studies __P__Bibliographies__P__Biographies____Popular Biographies
__P__Critical works about____Textbooks __P__Abstracts __P__Indexes
__P__Directories __P__Collected Works__P__Encyclopaedias ____Travel Lit.
____Juvenile Works ____No Limitations on Treatment of Subject

E. Formats of Publication or Reproduction:
__P__Monographs__P__Periodicals__P__Serials__S__Govt. Pubs.
__S__Reprints (have orig.) _P__Reprints (lack orig.)____Maps
____Atlases__P__Festschriften__S__Theses(USC)____Theses(non-USC)
_P___Diss. (USC) __S__Diss. (non-USC)____Newspapers__P__Learned Society Pubs.
__P__Pamphlets____Posters____Newsletters____Press Releases
____Ephemera____Broadsides____Manuscripts____Archival Collections
____Other Special Collections____Artists Books
____Scripts____Auction Catalogs____Exhibition Catalogs____Corp. Annual Reports
____Architectural Drawings____Realia ____Scores
____Slides__P__Microfilm__P__Microfiche____Microprint
____Microcards__S__Audio Cassettes____Compact Discs (Audio)
____Laser Discs (Video)____CD-ROM (Databases, etc.)__S__Video Tapes
____LP's____Photographic Prints____Photographic Negatives
____Software____Other Machine-Readable Data Files____Other Formats
____No Limitations on Format of Publication or Reproduction

F. Date of Publication or Reproduction:
____Current Pubs. Only--No Retrospective__X__No Limitations on Date of Publication
____Retrospective Only ____Current Pubs. Plus Highly Selective Retrospective
____Emphasis on Materials Published Since:_____

G. Attach Separate Sheet/Expand Online Entry if Certain Presses, Printers, Publishers, Organizations, or Issuing Agencies Are Emphasized in Collecting for this Subject:

* * *

P = primary

S = secondary

III. COLLECTION DESCRIPTION AND POLICIES

A. Library Selector(s) Responsible for This Subject:
Ruth Wallach

B. Faculty/Library Liaison for This Subject:
Barrie Thorne

C. Level of Collecting Intensity by Detailed Subject Subdivisions:
[L.C. class range in brackets on line after subject subdivision:]

	Conspectus Values		
	ECS	CCI	DCI
Anthropology [GN479-GV1000]	2	1	3
Biography, diaries, memoirs [CT3200-3900]	2	1	4
History [D600-E600]	2	2	4
Classics, literature [PA, PG2900-PT5000]	2	2	4
Communications/Linguistics [P94-P120]	1	1	3
Economics/Politics/Law [HD6050-6220, HQ1000-1870, HX546, JF847-855, JK1800-JN, JX1965]	1	1	3
Psychology [BF692]	2	2	3
Feminism and feminist theory [HQ1000-HQ1870]	2	2	4
Sociology/social issues [HN49-HQ1000, H6550-6626]	2	2	4
Philosophy/Religion/Mythology [B105-BX8000]	2	2	4

D. Summary Statement:

The Department for the Study of Women and Men in Society (SWMS) is a fast growing, extremely diverse department. It offers coursework in Anglo-American literature, as well as comparative literature, sociology, communications, feminist theory, politics and economics, history, and physical education. Because of the broad appeal of the subject area, it is especially difficult to create a good library collection to support SWMS. Although many other disciplines besides SWMS cover some of the subject subdivisions (for example, history, philosophy, etc.), a comprehensive literature coverage remains to be achieved.

The library collection has many of the classic 20th century feminist studies, and can, therefore, maintain undergraduate education in that area. Recently, an effort has been undertaken to develop a collection focusing on feminist perspective in world history, politics and literature, as these areas constitute the main thrust of SWMS curriculum. A major problem is financing a well developed collection. Although many of the sources are acquired through funds other than SWMS (as mentioned above), the SWMS department has identified around 60 relevant journal publications, only 9 of which are collected within the USC Library system. The titles of the journals are listed below. As the Library cannot afford to subscribe to these publications, an effort has been made to galvanize the acquisition of monographic material.

There are many important microform collections of papers dealing with the history of feminist thought. These are very expensive, and are scattered throughout the United States. A special effort should be made to maintain strong cooperative agreements with other research libraries that have better collections in women's studies.

If and when the SWMS department establishes a Ph.D. program, the library will have to reconsider its collection policy. Developing a good women's and gender studies collection is imperative, as this field is becoming increasingly important in academic studies.

The following is a list of serial publications submitted to the library by the department for the Study of Women and Men in Society. These publications are not collected by the Library system:

On campus with women (newsletter from American Council on Education, Project on the Status and Education of Women)
Barnard College, occasional papers on women's issues
Changing men
Feminist review
Gender and Society
Journal of women's history
men's studies review
NWSA journal
New directions for women
Resources for feminist research (RFR/DRF)
Trivia
Woman's building newsletter
Women's studies quarterly
Differences
Genders
Sage: a scholarly journal on black women
Feminist teacher
Feminist collections
Gender and history
Out/look: national lesbian and gay quarterly
Empathy
Affilia: journal of women and social work
Women: a cultural review
Journal of gender studies
Journal of women and aging
Gender and Society
Camera obscura: journal of feminism and film theory
NWSA journal
Women and language
Conditions
Lesbian ethics
Sinister wisdom
Women's studies abstracts
Heresies
Tulsa studies in women's literature
U.S.-Japan women's journal
Journal of the history of sexuality
Belles letres: a review of books by women
Ikon
Journal of feminist studies in religion

Lilith: the Jewish women's magazine
Sojourner
Calyx
ISIS: women's international cross-cultural exchange
Manushi
Media report to women
Psychology of women quarterly
Women of power
Women and politics
Women's studies in communication
Women's studies librarian
Yale journal of law and feminism
Harvard women's law journal
Women and criminal justice
Women and therapy
Journal of feminist family therapy

E.   Other Collection Policy Statements Related to This Subject:

F.   Summary of Corresponding Lines in the Conspectus for This Subject: ANT46 - ANT116
AUX26
ECO49, 49.11, 49.14
ECO87.10 - ECO92.32
ECO197.03 - ECO107.04
HIS26-HIS534.10
LLL7.10 - LLL422.15
PAR2.10 - PAR418.10
POL14.10, 83, 241.10
PSY35, 52

G.   Subject is Collected Primarily in These USC Libraries/Collections:
__X__DML_____Acctg_____Am.Lit.__X__Arch._____Boeck. __X__Cinema/TV
__X_Coll _____Crocker_____Dental___E. Asian__X__Educ._X___Gero.
_____GovDocs_____Hanck._____Hoose__X__Law__X__Medical ____Microg.
__X__Music_____Schoen._____Sci. __X__SocWork_____SpecColl__X__VKC

H.   Overlap Statement:

I.   Other Campus Library Resources Outside of Central Library System:
The departmental library, which is primarily concerned with current journals.

J.   Other Regional Library Resources Available in This Subject:
UCLA

K.   Cooperative Collection Development Agreements in Force:

* * *

IV. ACQUISITION, BUDGETARY, AND PRESERVATION INFORMATION

A. Primary Means of Acquisition for This Subject:
_P___Individual Item Purchase __P__Broad Subject Approval Plans _____Country Approval Plan _P___Specialized Subject Approval Plan _____Specialized Subject/Country Approval Plan_____Publisher Approval Plan__P__Standing Order _____Membership _____Depository Agreements_____Blanket Order__P__Subscription____Special Arrangements with Vendor/Publisher _____Gift _____Mailing List _____Exchange _____ _____

B. Fund Numbers and Current FY Allocations:
1. Regular Fund:_____D2660_____/__$_1819_____

C. Previous FY Expenditures:
1. Approval & Other On-Behalf-Of Expenditures
   A. Regular Approval Expenditures:$_____
   B. Other On-Behalf-Of Expenditures:$_____

2. Regular Fund:$_____/%Books_____
   $_____ %Serials_____
   (Serials)
   $_____ %Other_____
   (Other)

3. Special Fund: $_____/%Books_____
   (Monographs)
   $_____ /%Serials_____
   (Serials)
   $_____ /%Other_____
   (Other)

D. Preservation Needs Assessment for This Subject:

__X___Low _____Medium _____High

E. Preservation Priority Status for This Subject:

__X___Low _____Medium _____High

F. Previous FY Preservation Expenditures for This Subject:

$_____

UNIVERSITY OF WASHINGTON LIBRARIES   UWA 1

Operations Manual

Policies, Guidelines and Procedures

Vol. IV
Section B
Part VII Ethnic/Women
 Studies Fund Group
5. Women Studies

DRAFT

COLLECTION DEVELOPMENT STATEMENT   SUBJECT: Women Studies

PRINCIPAL SELECTOR: Cynthia Fugate   DATE: March 1984

1.   SUBJECT DEFINITION.

    a.   General statement.

        Women Studies is an interdisciplinary subject and includes, but is not
        limited to, the study of women in history, politics, present day society
        and culture, and the arts.

    b.   Subject classification analysis.

        1.   Library of Congress Classification (LC)

            Books on women appear primarily in the H classification, social
            sciences, with allied material in B, philosophy, psychology,
            religion; J, political science; N, fine arts; and P, language and
            literature. Materials on women appear in many of the other
            classifications.

        2.   Dewey Decimal Classification.

            Materials on women are found mainly in the 300's: 301.4, women's
            history; 331.4, employment of women; 324.3, suffrage, and 396, women.
            Books on the psychology of women are classified under 155.6, and those
            on the anthropology of women under 572.9. The 800's, literature, and
            900's, history, also contain materials on women.

2.   DEPARTMENT STATEMENT.

    Women Studies is an interdisciplinary program. A Bachelor of Arts degree with a
    concentration in Women Studies is offered through General Studies. Graduate
    students in other fields may write theses or dissertations on aspects of women
    studies, and the Women Studies faculty serve on doctoral committees for
    candidates in English history, philosophy, and other disciplines. Women Studies
    499 attracts graduate students from a variety of disciplines; Women Studies 533,
    a graduate level seminar, is offered periodically. The Women Studies Program
    has established the Northwest Center for Research on Women with a National
    Endowment for the Humanities grant to support scholars doing graduate level
    research.

3.   SCOPE.

    a.   Chronologic

        No period is excluded; emphasis is on the 19th and 20th centuries.

    b.   Geographic.

        There are no geographic exclusions. The collection includes materials on
        women related to all subjects with emphasis on women in the United States,
        Canada, and Western Europe. As materials become available, future

UNIVERSITY OF WISCONSIN - MADISON
MEMORIAL LIBRARY

Collection Development Guidelines:
Women's Studies (Social Sciences)

Third revision, March 1992

Scholarly context

Women's studies is an interdisciplinary field that examines
women's experiences and gender roles as they affect the lives of
women and men, human culture, and the course of history. Most
women's studies scholarship is informed by a feminist
perspective.

Institutional context

Memorial Library supports the curriculum of the Women's Studies
Program, which includes an undergraduate major, a certificate,
and a graduate minor. The library also undergirds the research
projects of the Women's Studies Research Center and supports
scholarship on women and gender roles in a wide range of
university departments.

Division of responsibilities

The Women's Studies Bibliographer is responsible for collecting
English-language print materials relating to women's studies in
the social sciences. Print materials typically include
monographs, periodicals, serials, newspapers, pamphlets, and
selected U.S. and international documents. The Women's Studies
Bibliographer is also responsible for collecting microform,
audiovisual, and electronic materials.

The Humanities bibliographers and the Area Studies bibliographers
are responsible for women's studies materials in their own areas
of subject and/or language expertise.

Other campus libraries also support women's studies in the social
sciences. The State Historical Society is the library of record
for American women's history and thus supports the graduate
program in Women's History administered by the History
Department. The Middleton Health Sciences Library serves the
large enrollments in such courses as "Women and Their Bodies in
Health and Disease." The College Library maintains a Women's
Studies Reading Area with books (primarily paperbacks) on women's
issues, current issues of selected magazines and journals, and
vertical files of clippings and pamphlets.

Memorial Library is the library of record for interdisciplinary
works of feminist scholarship, and for specialized materials in
the social sciences not more appropriately housed at member

General women studies   C

Women in the Pacific Northwest   B

Library serve as referral points for materials which complement the resources available at the University of Washington.

The Library of the University of Oregon, Eugene, supports a major Women's Studies Program recently established at that institution.

c.   Cooperative loan arrangements.

The Center for Research Libraries serves as an extension of the Women Studies collection for expensive microform sets, including archival material, infrequently used research journals, foreign dissertations, and newspapers.

d.   Cooperative acquisitions projects.

Recommendations for purchase of very expensive, or low use research materials may be made to the Center for Research Libraries.

7.   OTHER.

a.   Computerized databases.

Materials on women studies can be found in most of the social sciences databases available at the Suzzallo Library, such as ERIC and Sociological Abstracts, as well as on MEDLINE and other databases available at the Health Sciences Library.

b.   Specific features.

Women Studies is a highly interdisciplinary Program which relies heavily on library materials acquired by many selectors for other subject collections such as anthropology, English, the health sciences, history, etc. The primary concerns of the Women Studies selector are to acquire the interdisciplinary works in the field which are too broad for other collections, and to keep selectors informed about material in their areas which is needed for program support.

8.   COLLECTION LEVELS.

The general collection level supports the course work of advanced undergraduate and master's degree programs, or sustained independent study of less than research intensity. It includes a wide range of basic monographs both current and retrospective, complete collections of the works of more important writers, selections from the works of secondary writers, a selection of representative journals, and the reference tools and fundamental bibliographical apparatus pertaining to the subject.

Comprehensive level	A
Research level	B
Study level	C
Basic level	D
Minimal level	E

selection will include more on minority women and women in developing countries.

c. Language.

English is the primary language, but the collection includes works in other Western European languages, primarily French and German.

d. Format.

Types of material in the collection include monographs, sets, serials, microforms, reprints, reference works, and audiovisual materials.

e. Exclusions.

There are no exclusions.

4. LOCATION STATEMENT.

The Women Studies collection is housed primarily in the Suzzallo Library, with supplementary and some duplicate works in the Odegaard Undergraduate Library. Within Suzzallo, books are shelved in the main stacks, journals are in the Periodicals Collection, and microforms are in the Microforms-Newspapers Section. The Reference Division, the Government Publications Division and the Archives and Manuscripts Division all contain important relevant material. Materials of interest to students of women studies may also be found at the Art, Business Administration, Drama, Philosophy, and Social Work Libraries.

5. SYSTEM COORDINATION.

It is the primary responsibility of the principal selector for women studies to see that the collection includes important books, periodicals, reference works, and special microform documents dealing specifically with women. Because of their interdisciplinary nature, most of these materials are actually acquired by other selectors, including but not limited to the Undergraduate Library as well as anthropology, education, history, the several literatures collected, political science, and sociology. Material on women's health, women in the health professions, and in the history of medicine is acquired by the Health Sciences Library.

6. RESOURCE SHARING.

a. Related University of Washington information sources.

A small departmental collection of books, newsletters, newspapers and a few journals is located at the Women Studies Office in Padelford. A collection of current paperbacks and newspaper clippings is available at the Library in the Women's Information Center in Cunningham Hall. The Women's Commission Office, 201 HUB, maintains a file of current newsletters and some books.

b. Related local and regional collections.

The collections of the Washington State Library and the Seattle Public

libraries. Through Wisconsin Interlibrary Services (WILS) and
the office of the UW System Women's Studies Librarian, Memorial
Library's collection serves as a resource for women's studies
programs throughout the UW System.

Subject scope

Among the <u>areas emphasized</u> are:

Feminist theory (including critiques of social, political,
philosophical, and scientific theories of women's nature and
women's studies).

Studies of the intersection of gender with race, class,
ethnicity, sexual preference, and other "differences" (including
contemporary materials on women of color and other minority women
in the United States, historical and contemporary studies of
minority women in other nations and regions, lesbian studies).

Economics (including research on occupational sex segregation,
the role of women in developing economies, women's experiences in
the workforce and in labor organizations, women's unwaged labor).
[H, especially HD 6050 - HD 6223]

Sociology (including the study of women in self-selected and
socially-defined groups -- e.g., women's clubs, feminist
organizations, older women, minority women, housewives, women of
various classes, women of various regions, lesbians; the study of
social problems affecting women -- e.g., prostitution, rape,
battering, incest; and the choices women make that affect their
lives as citizens -- e.g., sexuality, marriage, childcare). The
Social Work Library also bears responsibility in this area.
[H, especially HQ 1075 - HQ 2030]

Psychology (including studies of sex role socialization, sex
differences in behavior, psychopathology.) The Social Work
Library also bears responsibility in this area.
[BF, especially BF 692.2 - BF 692.5]

Education (including examinations of girls' and women's education
historically and in the present, the roles of women in higher
education, sex equity in the college classroom). The
Instructional Materials Center also bears responsibility in this
area.
[L, especially LC 1401 - LC 2751]

Political science (including studies of sex differences in
political participation and attitudes, women's roles in electoral
politics and political movements).
[J]

History (including general works on women's history; works on
women's experiences in specific regions, countries, or periods;
histories of subjects primarily concerned with women, e.g.

housework). The State Historical Society bears full
responsibility for primary and secondary materials on American
women's history.
[C, especially CT 3200 - CT 3910;D]

Anthropology (including cross-cultural studies of women's
experience and roles, ethnographies focused on women and/or
gender divisions).
[G]

Health (including non-technical works on reproduction,
contraception, workplace hazards, substance abuse, etc., and
policy issues relevant to women's health). The Health Sciences
Library and the Social Work Library share responsibility in this
area.
[R]

Linguistics (including sex differences in language use and
nonverbal communication, non-sexist language reform).
[P]

Biography and autobiography (including women notable for
achievements in fields collected by the Women's Studies
Bibliographer; and non-literary diaries, journals, and letters by
women).

Bibliography
[Z, especially Z 7961 - Z 7965]

Among the areas selectively collected are:

Religion (including only works of greater interest as expressions
of the feminist movement than as scholarly studies of religion).
[BL - BX]

Science (including only feminist critiques of scientific theory
and practice, and the current status of women in the sciences).
[Q, especially Q 130; R; T]

Sports
[GV]

Among the areas not collected by the Women's Studies
Bibliographer are:

Belles lettres.
[PA - PZ]

Literary history, biography, and criticism.
[PA - PZ]

Fine arts, art history, and criticism.
[M; N]

Any materials in language other than English.

Popular materials, except when they serve as primary documents
for women's studies research (e.g., self-help books).

Philosophy and theology, except works falling under the rubric of
feminist theory.
[B - BD; BH - BX]

General works on sexuality.
[HQ 12 - HQ 471]

Professional materials in such areas as law, social work, and
medicine.

Works on American women in subject areas covered by the State
Historical Society Library.
[E; F]

Works for or about female-intensive professions (e.g., nursing
teaching, librarianship) except when informed by a feminist
perspective and not within the scope of another campus library.

Notes

This document delineates the scope of responsibility of the
Women's Studies Bibliographer. Most of the subject areas listed
as "not collected" or "selectively collected" are covered by
other bibliographers within Memorial Library (e.g., feminist
theology, the history of women in science, literary criticism) or
by member libraries (e.g., women in the arts). Overall, the
General Library System aims for a balanced collection in women's
studies to support the broad spectrum of research and teaching
interests at UW-Madison.

In addition to academic and trade publications, the Women's
Studies Bibliographer collects representative small press books
and periodicals to serve as primary sources for the study of
women's experiences and to reflect a wide array of feminist and
anti-feminist analysis. The State Historical Society shares
responsibility for the acquisition of "alternative" periodicals
by and about women.

Susan E. Searing
Women's Studies Bibliographer

San Diego State — UC San Diego

MEMORANDUM OF AGREEMENT: WOMEN AND GENDER JOURNALS AND MONOGRAPHS

The goal of this agreement is to ensure that major journals and monographs in the field of Women and Gender Studies are available to scholars and students at San Diego State University and the University of California, San Diego.

The scope of this agreement includes the journals of women and gender in the attached list. Both campuses have full access to these journals and books through interlibrary loan. Occasional special requests to borrow complete issues or bound volumes will be considered.

It also includes collaboration on the acquisition and retention of Women and Gender Studies monographs in these designated areas.

    a.   UC San Diego agrees to purchase monographs covering women and gender in Great Britain and the Commonwealth, both historical and current, to support doctoral level study and research.

    b.   San Diego State University Library agrees to purchase monographs covering women and gender in family issues, psychology and social work to support their Master's level programs.

ADDITIONAL COMMITMENTS:

    1.   Processing and retention are the responsibilities of the holding libraries.

    2.   All serial titles are to be retained permanently by the library that owns them. However, holding campuses have the option of retaining issues unbound, binding them, converting them to microform, and/or transferring older volumes/issues to storage. Costs associated with retention are borne by the holding campuses.

3. Through a process of consulting with one another, the holding libraries may make changes in the journals list as cessations occur, journals are not found useful, etc.

4. This agreement does not forbid either library from using its own funds to acquire materials that are judged to be needed on site for primary users.

5. Either participant wishing to withdraw from or significantly alter their participation in this agreement must notify the other in writing of the intention at least one calendar year in advance.

6. Although it is assumed that this agreement will be in force indefinitely, the participants will review the agreement every two years. The first review is scheduled for July 1993. Significant changes in the agreement must be negotiated by both participants.

SIGNATURES OF THE UNIVERSITY LIBRARIANS OF THE PARTICIPATING LIBRARIES:

_____
Dorothy Gregor
University of California,
San Diego

Date: July 11, 1991

_____
Don Bosseau
San Diego State University

Date: _____

UC-Stanford Women's Studies Collection Development Consortium

Statement of Purpose and Goals

The UC-Stanford Women's Studies Collection Development Consortium is composed of librarians from the UC campuses and Stanford University who are responsible for developing and managing collections in women's studies. Our purpose is to collaborate and to coordinate efforts in acquiring and providing access to women's studies materials throughout the consortium. Research and teaching in women's studies are expanding at a rapid rate on all campuses. Significant publishing growth combined with shrinking acquisition budgets makes collaboration and resource sharing imperative in order to assure adequate coverage of the discipline and access to library resources and materials.

Our goals include the following:

1. To develop formal collaborative collection development agreements based on programmatic needs and strengths of individual campuses.

2. To make policy recommendations regarding issues related to collection development, management, evaluation, and access such as ILL and processing of shared purchase sets. To develop guidelines and procedures for major projects, e.g. implementation of the Women's Studies Conspectus and the acquiring and sharing of Audio/Visual materials.

3. To coordinate projects and make policy recommendations related to serial selections, cancellations, and access, e.g. the UC-Stanford List of Women's Studies Periodicals.

4. To coordinate the acquisition and location of microform sets.

   a. To develop and present SCAP proposals agreed upon by the consortium members.
   b. To produce union lists in order to facilitate access to these research materials.

5. To promote adequate and timely bibliographic access through MELVYL and other systems.

6. To work with microform publishers to develop resources and purchasing arrangements that suit our users needs and are adaptable to both individual campus budgets and SCAP purchases.

7. To promote the exchange and development of instructional tools and checklists to aid research in women's studies.

8. To identify preservation needs and coordinate preservation projects related to women's studies.

Feb. 7, 1992

RLG CONSPECTUS®

WOMEN'S STUDIES

Prepared by
Sarah M. Pritchard, The Library of Congress*
under the auspices of the RLG Collection Management and Development Committee

Approved: January, 1990

* The author is currently Associate Executive Director, The Association of Research Libraries.

CONTENTS

I.   Introduction

The RLG Conspectus is an approach to the evaluation of library collections by subject. Its detailed structure and cooperative elements may also aid in prospective collection development, bibliographic instruction, faculty liaison and collaborative programs. The women's studies component of the conspectus is intended to reflect the field at its broadest, encompassing the humanities, social sciences and sciences, and covering both historical and contemporary aspects of the collection. The nature of the subject is such that the scope of research and the variety of primary, secondary and bibliographic sources available are constantly growing and changing, thus, the women's studies conspectus must be treated as an evolving document. Librarians working with it are urged to check for the existence of new tools and the emergence of new research trends, and not to limit themselves only to those listed herein.

The women's studies conspectus is composed of two parts, the narrative guidelines and the listing of conspectus "lines" by subject and classification number. The narrative is considered a supplement to the lines, which themselves become part of the full Conspectus database maintained by RLG. Although the lines are most commonly defined by Library of Congress classification, the goal of the conspectus methodology is to evaluate subject areas, not particular classes. Not every specific classification or subject term related to women's studies will be found incorporated into the lines, because many are too narrow to be construed as a separate area of collection development. The conspectus lines are not intended to support searching for detailed subject information, and in such cases the conspectus should be used in conjunction with other reference tools.

This conspectus would not exist without the initiative, support and expertise of the librarians in the Women's Studies Section of the Association of College and Research Libraries. They first suggested it to the RLG committee in 1984 and continued to work on the issue and serve as a review group through its completion. Ruth Dickstein, WSS member and librarian at the University of Arizona, assisted in the development of the classification lines by sharing her work on *Women in LC's Terms*, for which advance galleys were graciously provided by Oryx Press. Field testing of the Conspectus was done at Princeton University, Emory University, New York University and Sarah Lawrence College. The author expresses appreciation to all of the librarians who assisted in the development and testing, to the Conspectus Subcommittee of the RLG Collection Management and Development Committee, and to the RLG staff for their interest, encouragement and practical assistance.

II.   Overview of Women's Studies

Women's studies comprises the academic study of women and gender across all subjects; feminism as a multi-faceted, multicultural international movement addressing a wide range of social, political, and economic issues; and feminist critique and theory not only related to women but to general academic subjects and contemporary concerns. Women's studies is highly interdisciplinary and draws on a variety of sources and methods. Although regarded at first as a social science, women's studies has made contributions in all domains from the narrow study of women as an aspect of traditional categories of scholarship, to a feminist critique of knowledge that calls for a restructuring of all intellectual analysis. Libraries in institutions without women's studies programs still need collections in this field to support research in history, literature, philosophy, and social and political sciences. The following two texts give good summaries of women's studies: Sheila Ruth, *Issues in Feminism: A First Course in Women's Studies* and *Women's Realities, Women's Choices: An Introduction to Women's Studies*, edited by the Hunter College Women's Studies Collective.[*]

---

[*] A bibliography of all specialized sources mentioned in these guidelines is appended.

The establishment of women's studies in American higher education dates from about 1970, and now supports research and instructional programs at the BA, MA, and PhD level. In developing particular collections, librarians must be aware of two complementary approaches in women's studies: to develop a separate, cohesive body of feminist theory and research about women, and also to transform the "mainstream" curriculum through integrating this theory and research into individual disciplines. An excellent survey of the evolving nature of women's studies programs and research is provided by Catharine Stimpson in *Women's Studies in the United States*, and by Marilyn Boxer's review essay in *Signs*, "For and About Women: The Theory and Practice of Women's Studies in the United States."

Topics related to women's history and literature, health, and contemporary women's social, economic and political issues are also covered in public, school, and special libraries to varying degrees. Library collections in women's studies may support, in addition to formal educational curricula, the needs of business, policy makers, community organizations, and the general public. Some examples of the broader use of women's studies materials in libraries are described in *Connecting Women in the Community: A Handbook for Programs*, by Joy C. Przestwor.

III.   Library Materials for Women's Studies

The breadth and interdisciplinarity of the field of women's studies as it is practiced in the United States is exemplified by the list of chapter headings in Catherine Loeb, Susan Searing, and Esther Stineman's *Women's Studies: A Recommended Core Bibliography, 1980-1985*:

Anthropology, Cross-Cultural Surveys, and International Studies
Art and Material Culture
Autobiography, Biography, Diaries, Memoirs, and Letters
Business, Economics, and Labor
Education and Pedagogy
History
Language and Linguistics
Law
Literature (divided by Drama, Essays, Fiction, History and Criticism, Mixed Genres, and Poetry)
Medicine, Health, Sexuality, and Biology
Politics and Political Theory
Psychology
Reference (Audiovisual, Bibliographies, Biographical Materials, and General)
Religion and Philosophy
Science, Mathematics, and Technology
Sociology and Social Issues
Sports
Women's Movement and Feminist Theory
Periodicals

Spanning and transcending the complete range of disciplines, women's studies draws on a rich, sometimes serendipitous or unlikely body of resources. With its origins in social activism, a tradition of reinterpreting existing canons and rediscovering overlooked evidence, a focus on integration and synthesis of formats and methods and a wide theoretical net, it is desirable to collect materials in all of the following categories:

1. A thorough collection of reference tools: indexes, bibliographies, directories, almanacs, dictionaries, biographical works, and works in library science;
2. Current academic and trade publishing: scholarly monographs, texts, anthologies, fiction and creative writings, and general or popular works;
3. Serial and monographic works from non-traditional sources: ephemeral, small press, activist, and ethnic materials;
4. Historical collections in history, science, and social sciences, not necessarily "feminist" in orientation but treating of women or traditional female concerns, or written by women even if not on the subject of women;
5. Foreign publications: historical and current works from Great Britain, Canada, and Europe; coverage of Africa, Asia, Latin America, Australia and the South Pacific, especially recent literature in politics, social sciences, and literature;
6. Periodicals: academic, activist, literary and popular magazines;
7. Documents from U.S. and foreign governments and from international organizations on public policy, law, development, health, education, and economics;
8. Working papers, conference papers, reports, syllabi and the like from academic and other kinds of organizations;
9. Non-print resources: microform sets; films, videotapes, music, sound recordings; access to databases in science, social science, and humanities, including non-bibliographic databases for statistical and demographic research.
10. Special collections: manuscripts, archival materials, posters, photographs, ephemera, diaries, correspondence, realia and popular culture materials.

IV.   Collection Evaluation in Women's Studies

This section lists tools evaluators may need in applying the conspectus or for other collection development work. It is arranged by types of materials rather than by collecting levels; full citations for women's studies sources are in the bibliography. When using bibliographies to compare holdings, spot-checking is appropriate as long as it is done evenly across relevant parts of the book.

1. *General tools and current collecting:*

Women's studies has benefited from the recent publication of several basic tools for collection development and evaluation. The best overview of the available resources is Joan Ariel's *Building Women's Studies Collections: A Resource Guide*. The first section of this guide lists basic bibliographies, guides, and indexes to the field. The most thorough and useful are Loeb; its predecessor *Women's Studies: A Recommended Core Bibliography* by Stineman and Loeb; Susan Searing's *Introduction to Library Research in Women's Studies*; and the extremely thorough 1987 edition of Patricia Ballou's *Women: A Bibliography of Bibliographies*. A narrative article on current collecting strategies was written by Ariel and Searing in *Selection of Library Materials in Applied and Interdisciplinary Fields*.

The most comprehensive continuing bibliography of English-language works in all areas of women's studies is *New Books on Women and Feminism*, issued twice yearly by the Office of the Women's Studies Librarian at the University of Wisconsin; it covers monographs, new serial titles, fiction and poetry, and audio-visual resources. Although now ceased, another useful comprehensive tool is *BiblioFem*, a microfiche publication of the combined library catalogs of the Fawcett Library and the Equal Opportunities Commission in Great Britain that appeared from 1978-1986. Both of these sources draw extensively on LC-MARC tapes, however, it is difficult to put in a meaningful direct order for LC bibliographic data since the field of women's studies necessitates so many class numbers and subject headings.

2. *Historical collections:*

To assess the strength of a collection for women's history in particular countries or times, consult the general sources in no. 1 above for various bibliographies. Two very broad, multi-diciplinary works are Virginia Terris' *Women in America* and the two-volume *Women and Society*, edited by Marie Rosenberg and others. Several library catalogs and microform bibliographies are helpful. The catalogs of the Schlesinger Library and the Sophia Smith Collection at Smith College and the microform publication *Bibliography of American Women* constitute good lists for American history. *BiblioFem* is excellent for general history and for British and Commonwealth countries. The bibliography accompanying the *Gerritsen Collection of Women's History 1543-1945*, and the *Catalogue of the Library of the International Archives for the Women's Movement* give greater coverage for Western European women's historical sources. The published LC shelflist can help with many historical areas.

The interdisciplinary and revisionist trends of women's history make it difficult to define all the primary sources necessary to feminist studies. In general, a good historical collection including educational writings, textbooks, housekeeping manuals, medical works on women, conduct and advice books, religious literature, social and political philosophy, economic and labor history, travel narratives, government documents and belles lettres will support historical research in women's studies.

3. *Periodicals:*

The longest running index is *Women Studies Abstracts*; it covers journals in women's studies and selected articles from other more general periodicals. Women's studies research will draw on major indexes in other fields such as *Psychological Abstracts*, the *Social Sciences Citation Index*, *Art Index*, *America: History and Life*, etc. Again, strong collections in the social sciences and humanities will provide a good base. Essential women's studies and feminist periodicals including those from small presses are covered by the quarterly "current contents" publication *Feminist Periodicals*, the *Alternative Press Index*, and by the recently ceased but still valuable *Annotated Guide to Women's Periodicals in the United States and Canada*, edited by Terry Mehlman. Loeb, Ariel, and Searing all contain good lists of titles, as does *Magazines for Libraries*. Clare Potter's *Lesbian Periodicals Index* is valuable for historical and current documentation in this important, often ephemeral literature up to 1980. Libraries supporting research or programs in contemporary feminism may need to join various organizations to receive major newsletters in the field.

British, Irish, and Commonwealth periodicals are covered by Doughan and Sanchez, *Feminist Periodicals, 1855-1984*. Current European periodicals are listed in *Women's Studies in Western Europe* by Stephen Lehmann and Eva Sartori, and in the relatively new British publication *Studies on Women Abstracts*. Historical periodicals are listed in the Gerritsen Collection (above) and the *History of Women* microform set from Research Publications, and in *Women's Periodicals and Newspapers from the Eighteenth Century to 1981*, edited by James P. Danky. For non-Western countries periodical coverage can be difficult to evaluate and relies to a great extent on government and international organization publications and trade and academic sources that are sometimes short-lived.

4. *Special subjects and area studies:*

To evaluate the collection in selected subjects (e.g., art, education, psychology, health, religion, ethnic groups) at a greater level of detail than is provided in general bibliographies, consult the numerous specialized bibliographies as listed in Ballou, Loeb, and Searing.

These basic reference works should also be the starting point for area studies bibliographies, to evaluate holdings about women in a particular region or country. Guides covering more than one country include Pamela Byrne, *Women in the Thirld World: A Historical Bibliography*; Fenton and Heffron, *Women in the Third World: A Directory of Resources*; and Frey, *Women in Western European History*.

The following titles focus on specific areas: Davis Bullwinkle, *African Women: A General Bibliography 1976-1985*, and his *Women of Northern, Western and Central Africa*; Lucie Cheng, *Women in China: Bibliography of Available English-Language Materials*, Karen Wei, *Women in China*; Samira Meghdessian, *Status of the Arab Woman*; Carol Sakala, *Women of South Asia*; Donita Simmons, *Women in the South Pacific*; and K. Lynn Stoner, *Latinas of the Americas: A Source Book*. Country holdings should span a range of subjects. For foreign language coverage of women's studies, see below.

In subject areas, online searches of the full MARC database using specific LC subject headings may yield useful bibliographies. For non-Western country studies, keyword searching is recommended and is a good way to verify a range of publications.

5. *Literary collections:*

This conspectus does not attempt to include call number lines for individual women writers, poets, and essayists. Libraries with special genre collections of women's fiction or poetry can rate them in the call number range closest to the proper literary period and country, and use the notes field to clarify holdings. For collections of women's literary writings, a large number of diverse sources and checklists may be needed. Among these are: Diva Daims and Janet Grimes, *Toward a Feminist Tradition: An Annotated Bibliography of Novels in English by Women, 1891-1920*; Janet Todd, *A Dictionary of British and American Women Writers, 1660-1800*; Boos and Todd, *Bibliography of Women and Literature*; Davis and Joyce, *Personal Writings by Women to 1900*; Joan Reardon and Kristine Thorsen, *Poetry by American Women, 1900-1975*; Narda Lacey Schwartz, *Articles on Women Writers*; Jeanette Foster, *Sex Variant Women in Literature*; Barbara Grier, *The Lesbian in Literature*; and Sharon Yntema, *More Than 100 Women Science Fiction Writers*.

For other countries and languages, if no separate bibliographies are available, use bibliographies appropriate to the literary output of that region in general supplemented by scholarly works on the history of women writers. Specific country coverage is provided by Brenda Berrian, *Bibliography of African Women Writers and Journalists*; Claire Mamola, *Japanese Women Writers in English Translation*; Elke Frederickson, *Women Writers of Germany, Austria, and Switzerland*; Debra Adelaide, *Australian Women Writers*; and Diane Marting, *Women Writers of Spanish America*. Also helpful is Resnick and de Courtivron, *Women Writers in Translation*. Consult Loeb, Ballou and Searing for additional sources.

6. *Foreign language collections:*

The bibliographic apparatus of women's studies is much more extensive in English than in other languages. Nonetheless, at the research and comprehensive collecting levels, foreign language resources are obligatory especially French, German, and Spanish. For current reference tools, publishers, and periodicals, consult Lehmann and Sartori (above). Some historical bibliographies are available, including the *Gerritsen Collection*; *Die Frauenfrage in Deutschland*; *Women in Western European History*; and the *Catalogue of the Library of the International Archives for the Women's Movement*.

For most non-European languages only scattered works are available and good current research coverage of a country is the best way to ensure women's studies holdings in that language. Area studies bibliographies with multi-lingual coverage on the subject of women in a particular region are recommended, selected use of general foreign-language national bibliographies. Printed and online LC catalog records include strong foreign-language coverage (use online searches with careful attention to date ranges in MARC).

7. *Smaller libraries:*

To evaluate smaller collections, the *abridgement* of Loeb (222 p.) is recommended, together with Anne Chapman's *Feminist Resources for Schools and Colleges*. The abridged Loeb has about 50%

of the citations in the full edition except for periodicals, where the percentage is much less. Collections aiming at curricular support at the secondary or basic college level may find useful works such as the bibliography included in *Women's Place in the Academy: Transforming the Liberal Arts Curriculum*, edited by Schuster and Van Dyne, and *Women in the World: Annotated History Resources for the Secondary Student*, edited by Lyn Reese and Jean Wilkinson. A series of brochures compiled for public libraries by the Committee on the Status of Women in Librarianship, *Your Library: A Feminist Resource* comprises ten lists of basic titles in women's studies, women's literature, lesbians, Black women, women in management, and other topics. With smaller collections where only a core women's studies collection is to be kept, it is essential to use the most up-to-date bibliographies possible, so the titles cited here should be supplemented or replaced if appropriate new works exist.

8. *Nonbook materials:*

In most cases specialized bibliographies exist for women's films, music, etc., and are listed in the basic sources listed above under IV.1. With so much material in this category unclassed, collection evaluators will have to work closely with other specialists in each area. Although the conspectus covers primarily classed collections, libraries are encouraged to use the notes fields under a general number (for example ML82) to indicate strong holdings of other formats. In music, basic discographies in popular and classical music are found in Block and Neuls-Bates' *Women in American Music; International Discography of Women Composers* by Aaron Cohen; and the current *Ladyslipper Catalog*. The most comprehensive list for films is Kaye Sullivan's *Films For, By and About Women* and its 1985 supplement, listing approximately 6,000 films. For large microform sets, a useful annotated guide is by Sarah Pritchard, *Women's Studies Resources in Microform at the Library of Congress*; for the constant flow of new materials, consult standard sources like *Microform Review*. An overview of databases and datasets is in *Building Women's Studies Collections*, although such sources are rapidly growing.

9. *Special collections:*

For unique holdings like manuscripts, archives, realia, photographs and some ephemera, particular guides cannot really help assess the strength of a collection as compared to some known amount of existing materials. It is best to consult a monograph, dissertation, or other definitive research work on the subject of the collection (e.g., a person, an organization, a time period) to assess whether the items constitute partial or complete sources necessary to that area of study.

V.   Scope of the Women's Studies Conspectus

Library classification systems have been criticized for their bias and omissions in areas related to women's studies. There are endless numbers for minor aspects of "women in" a given subject, while no separate classes are assigned for important areas of women's experience and feminist critique, which may be scattered among the numbers for the general field in question (for example biology). Interdisciplinary works are often classed in numbers that do not reflect their main research uses; titles considered closely related by scholars and critics are classed in widely differing numbers.

The goal of the conspectus is not to create a new system for classification or description in women's studies, nor to anticipate all possible future directions of the field, but to present a balanced view of the subject based on what has already been published, while retaining the structure and vocabulary most common in academic libraries in the U.S. Not every possible number or subject heading related to women has been included. Major areas of women's studies are covered in detail, and numerous tangential fields are outlined more broadly. This conspectus covers LC subject classes from B to Z. The largest amount of women's studies materials is found in HD, HQ, and P; secondary areas are in B, E, J, L, N, and R. Call number ranges and subject descriptors alone cannot ensure a thorough evaluation, and librarians working in this area must rely on additional reference sources as indicated in section IV. The emphasis must be on evaluating the collection in a given *subject*, and not in an exact classification; the classification is merely a device upon which to "hang" a definition of the subject in question.

1. *Relationship to Other Parts of the Conspectus:*

Because of the interdisciplinary focus of women's studies and the kinds of exclusions noted below, it is desirable to use the women's studies conspectus dynamically with other related sections of the conspectus. That is, this conspectus could be used to survey subject collections in other areas (e.g. literature, education), and other parts of the conspectus could be used for greater detail where the women's studies lines give only broad groupings (for example music or law). It would also be misleading to confine analysis of women's studies only to this conspectus and to ignore such analysis when evaluating holdings in other subjects. Identifiable overlap and/or subject relevance is found in the following areas of the conspectus as a whole:
- country and area studies: history, anthropology, literature, law, government documents
- humanities: fine and performing arts, religion
- social sciences: education, psychology, sociology, and anthropology
- science and technology: medicine, biology, technology

2. *Explanation of Numbers and Ranges:*

Classification numbers and ranges are included in the women's studies conspectus if they represent a major subject focus of the field, or a narrow subject closely related to a major area. If the LC shelflist showed very few books in a number that was not of major subject importance, it was either eliminated or combined into a broader group. Where it has been possible to verify current classificatory preferences, old or unused numbers have been omitted or a note added. In section VI below, problems and exclusions from this conspectus are listed for specific classes.

The entire number or range may apply to the specific subject descriptor (HD6095: Women's employment in the U.S.), or the range or grouping may represent a combining of numerous small subject areas, not necessarily consecutive, described in general by the subject label or labels (P96.S48, .S45, .S5: Sexism and sex roles in mass media). When there is no separate number for women's studies aspects, the number or class is for the broad area within which are important works; the subject descriptor then pinpoints the relevant topic ("BF: women and psychoanalysis;" "D802: Women in WWII resistance movements;" "PT5085-PT9556: Dutch and Scandinavian literatures--women, women authors, feminism"). Specific cutters (.W7) have not always been given where a range or group has been created. If a line has one of these broad ranges or single classification letters, the evaluation should be focused on how well that *subject* is represented as a whole; within the range or broader number, look only at the women's studies holdings reflected therein, not at the coverage of the general subject of the number. A subject bibliography may then be more helpful than trying to pinpoint exact call numbers.

If needed, more detailed classification breakdowns can be identified by using the LC class schedules. Searching one's own catalog or an online national database using LC subject headings will also identify call numbers for subjects where classification is scattered or inconsistent. A guide to both forms of access is *Women in LC's Terms: A Thesaurus of Library of Congress Subject Headings Relating to Women*, by Ruth Dickstein, Victoria Mills, and Ellen Waite. It includes an extensive list of subject headings and an appendix of class numbers, many too detailed or minor to constitute separate conspectus lines. Dickstein does not contain full classification schedules in all relevant areas, for example in class RG and in schedules using tables to build numbers based on geographic patterns (e.g. women's history, HQ1400+).

Lines have been designed for the overall subjects of each class and major subclass (e.g., "L: Women and Education"); some libraries may wish to use only these broad lines in areas where they have minimal holdings. RLG libraries are generally required to indicate values for all conspectus lines, but other local projects may vary in the degree of completion and detail needed. The broad lines may not be found as such in the online conspectus database.

3. *Vocabulary used for Subject Labels:*

Language structure, use, and terminology are fundamental concerns of women's studies research and feminist critique; LC terminology has been found lacking and alternatives have been proposed, most recently *A Women's Thesaurus*, edited by Mary Ellen Capek. In this conspectus the overriding principle has been to use terms from the vocabulary systems most in use in academic library cataloging and classification. The subject group labels used on the individual conspectus lines are a mix of keywords from the LC classification schedules, Library of Congress subject headings, and occasionally a phrase coined for this specific purpose.

The lines may not correspond exactly to the caption in the class schedule or the LCSH. Some lines have multiple terms in an attempt to convey the breadth of the topic as described in scholarly and reference works. If LC terminology is biased, out-of-date, or nonexistent, then new phrases have been used or added to the line, for example "women in Latin American literature." In most cases, older terms using "woman" have been changed to "women," even if the LC heading or caption itself has not officially changed. Users of the conspectus are encouraged to employ as many additional LC subject headings as may seem relevant when evaluating a particular area, since many books on similar subjects are given inconsistent classifications. When searching the conspectus online, librarians should keep in mind that complete LC subject headings have not been integrated into every line, so there may not be exact matches for a term listed in *LCSH*; searching will be most effective if keywords, synonyms and truncation are used.

VI.   Notes on Specific LC Classes

To help librarians when going through the conspectus, the following list explains particular omissions or other characteristics by LC class. In all cases, evaluators are encouraged to use the notes fields to adapt or explain their holdings if the lines do not apply exactly. Notes can also be used to indicate special collections, shared resources, and other local factors.

B: For attitudes toward women in Western philosophy, philosophy of feminism, feminist ethics, etc., see HQ. General psychology of women is in HQ, although feminist critiques of Freud, women and psychoanalysis, and detailed aspects of female psychology are scattered throughout BF.

C: Collective biography is also classed in HQ or by country (e.g. *Who's Who of American Women* is in E).

D: History of women by country is in HQ. Most wars have a subject subdivision for "women" or "women's work," but not all relevant books are in those numbers, for example, women resistors in WWII is with the general subject of underground movements. Individual numbers for collective biography, biography of queens, princesses, etc. are omitted. Some older general biography by country was classed in D, but most works are in HQ or CT.

E: Ethnic, Native American, and Afro-American women are classed here, with the general number for the minority group, and not in HQ. For women in U.S. wars, the same caution applies as in D above. Nurses and nursing in the Civil War is in R.

F: No lines for F are included here. Works on women in local U.S. state and city history are completely scattered among the numbers by place. History of women in Latin American countries is in HQ, except again local history such as women in Mexico City. Libraries with strong regional collections should use bibliographies or subject-heading searches to compare holdings.

G: Some possibly relevant anthropology and folklore headings have been omitted because they represent few works (anthropometry of women), are too general (folklore of marriage), or are not major areas identified with women's studies. Individual sports have not been separately listed.

HD: Individual occupations have not been separately listed; consult Dickstein or other supplemental sources to identify numbers.

HQ: Some numbers that still exist in the schedule but are little used for current classification have been omitted. Country numbers in HQ1400+ include both the general history and status of women, and feminist thought and movements in those countries.

J: There are numbers for women's suffrage and women in the civil service under each country; libraries with strengths in area studies should check schedules and use notes fields to identify.

K: As with J, only the general and United States class ranges have been listed here. The K conspectus and schedules (if they exist) may be used if more detailed holdings in women's legal status in other countries are to be evaluated.

L: LE-LG allow detailed numbers for women's colleges in each country; these are not listed in the Conspectus but may be added if relevant to a particular collection, or indicated in the notes.

M: Individual women composers and musicians are not classed together; musical compositions may be in unclassed collections but should be indicated in notes fields if holdings are strong.

N: Individual women artists, painters, and sculptors are not classed together. Bio-bibliographical guides exist to help identify a range of works if needed.

P: Lines for writings and criticism of individual authors are not included. To assess strong holdings of individual authors or groups of authors, consult supplemental tools and indicate in notes fields within the number ranges for women authors in that country/time period. Exact subject cutter numbers (e.g., ".W6") for "women in" the literature of a country/time period are not always given, especially on lines where several numbers are grouped; consult Dickstein or full schedules to identify.

Q: Feminist criticism of biology, primate studies, and other important philosophy of science is scattered among various numbers.

R: Clinical areas have been excluded; emphasis should be on historical studies, social aspects, status of women in the field, women as patients, and philosophical critiques.

S: Women in agricultural work (important in the literature of developing countries) is in HD. The subject of women farmers is scattered in S; use subject searches or supplemental sources.

T: In TR, books of photography of women (as subjects) have not been included. Women photographers are not classed as a group by LC.

Z: Detailed breakdown of women's studies bibliography is not given; consult schedules or reference sources. Lines are given for women's studies topics outside of Z7961-7965.

VII.   Assigning Conspectus Ratings

Numerical values in the conspectus are assigned for ECS, existing collection strength, and CCI, current collecting intensity. The following instructions apply:

1. These values decribe collections *absolutely*, not relatively. They should reflect a national perspective and broad cognizance of all facets of collecting as described in Section II.

2. When the value describes existing collection strength, it should reflect what is actually on the shelves. Shelflist measurement should *rarely* be used to assess strength in women's studies. Important bodies of research may be scattered among several numbers, any one number may not

be entirely related to women's studies, and ranges with few titles may still reflect comprehensive holdings. Use bibliographic tools as primary guides.

3. Spot-checking or sampling of bibliographies is generally recommended when comparing holdings; titles should be selected evenly from the relevant portions of the source work.

4. When assigning a value for a number or range that is not exclusively for a women's studies topic, base ratings only on the portion of the collection within that call number or range that is devoted to women's studies, not on the strength of the holdings in the broader topic.

5. When the value describes current collecting intensity, it represents *actual collecting practices*, and not *policy*, if that policy is being imperfectly observed.

6. Libraries are encouraged to use the "notes" field on individual conspectus lines to further describe local conditions, archival and special collections, vertical file holdings, non-print formats, and other resources that may clarify the assignment of ECS/CCI levels.

7. Language suffixes should be added as follows:
   E: primarily English-language material
   F: selected foreign-language material
   W: wide selection of foreign-language material
   Y: material primarily in one foreign language

These guidelines are intended to assess collecting levels for women's studies as a core subject at levels 1 and 2, and to be applied in accord with local emphasis to broader or more specialized strengths at the higher levels. Each level of collecting is presumed to be inclusive of those preceding it.

0. Out of scope: The library does not collect in this area. Given the nature of women's studies, even a very specialized library will find some areas within its scope; this value should be used on a line-by-line basis.

1. Minimal level: A subject area in which few selections are made beyond very basic works. Biographical dictionaries, survey texts (Ruth, Hunter College Collective), basic guides to the subject (Loeb, Searing, Stineman), almanacs, and selected works on current women's issues should be available. About 25% of the works listed in Chapman and in COSWL's *Your Library: A Feminist Resource* should be held. Core collections in history, literature, and the social sciences should include representative works in women's studies.

2. Basic Information Level: A collection of up-to-date general materials that serves to introduce and define the subject and to indicate the varieties of information available elsewhere. Good coverage of reference sources should include almanacs, general bibliographies, historical surveys, anthologies, biographical dictionaries, survey texts, selected editions of important works, and some major periodical titles. One-half of the works listed in Chapman, COSWL, Schuster and Van Dyne, and the abridged Loeb (or 25% of the full Loeb). About 35% of the works listed in *Books for College Libraries*.

3. Instructional Support Level: A collection that is adequate to support undergraduate and most graduate instruction, or sustained independent study; that is, adequate to maintain knowledge of a subject required for limited or generalized purposes, of less than research intensity. A strong reference collection is essential. Both materials necessary for women's studies courses, and for integrating feminist critique and women's studies topics into other disciplines, should be included. The 1988 edition of *Books for College Libraries*, and Jeanne Dost's *Women Studies Bibliography* have good coverage of women's studies at this level (consult *BCL* indexes since

citations are scattered). At least 3/4 of the materials listed in Loeb (complete ed.) and Stineman should be available; at least half of those in Rosenberg's *Women and Society*; a majority of the periodicals listed in *Women Studies Abstracts* and *Magazines for Libraries*; access to databases in the humanities and social sciences; current and some historical works in major European languages. Older material is retained for historical studies. Film and audio-visual resources may be important at this level. Segments of larger special collections (e.g. archives, manuscripts, photographs) may be considered in assessing strength at this level in particular topics.

4. Research Level: A collection that includes the major published source materials required for dissertations and independent research, works in many specialized and tangential areas, conference reports, broad foreign language holdings, imprints from all major world regions, small press, and selected ephemera. Extensive vertical file holdings may be needed to achieve research level holdings in specific topics. A strong collection of periodicals including academic, activist, and international publications. Large microform collections such as the *Gerritsen Collection*, *History of Women*, film of 19th-century periodicals, manuscripts of individuals and organizations, and oral history transcripts. Significant holdings of older materials and government documents, and research-level collections in history, literature, and social sciences. Music, audio-visual resources, manuscripts, and other special collections are essential for research level in some subjects and should be included on lines wherever relevant. Virtually all of the works listed in Loeb, Stineman, and Searing should be held; a large portion of the works in the two-volume *Women and Society* by Rosenberg et al; as many of the periodicals in *Women Studies Abstracts*, *Feminist Periodicals*, and *Magazines for Libraries* as possible, as well as serials no longer published. The broadest definitions of women's studies and feminist critique should be adopted.

5. Comprehensive Level: A collection in which a library endeavors, so far as is reasonably possible, to include all significant works of recorded knowledge (publications, manuscripts, and other forms), in all applicable languages, for a necessarily defined and limited field. This level of collecting intensity is one that maintains a "special collection;" the aim, if not the achievement, is exhaustiveness in subject and format. As many works as possible as listed in *BiblioFem* and *New Books on Women and Feminism*. Older material is retained and out-of-print works actively sought after. Every attempt is made to acquire, both currently and retrospectively, all relevant monographs, periodical titles, and microform sets. The collection will include, as appropriate, rare and limited editions, ephemeral material, vertical file holdings, underground and radical press, non-print materials of all kinds, dissertations, manuscripts and archives, unpublished papers and organizational documents, film and photographs, and similar types of materials. A comprehensive collection on women in one country or region would endeavor to collect exhaustively on all aspects (i.e. across numerous call number areas) of women's history and status in that region and in the feminist critique of that region's culture.

VIII.   Bibliography for Women's Studies Conspectus

This includes all specialized women's studies publications mentioned in the guidelines for the conspectus. Standard reference sources and indexes cited are not listed.

Adelaide, Debra. *Australian Women Writers: A Bibliographical Guide.* London: Pandora, 1988.

Ariel, Joan, ed. *Building Women's Studies Collections: A Resource Guide.* CHOICE Bibliographical Essay Series, no. 8. Middletown, CT: CHOICE, 1987.

Ariel, Joan and Susan Searing. "Women's Studies." In *Selection of Library Materials in Applied and Interdisciplinary Fields,* ed. Beth J. Shapiro and John Whaley, pp. 250-269. Chicago: American Library Association, 1987.

Arthur and Elizabeth Schlesinger Library on the History of Women in America. *The Manu-script Inventories and Catalogs of Books and Periodicals.* 10 v. Boston: G.K. Hall, 1983.

The Author, Subject, and Manuscript Catalogs of the Sophia Smith Collection, (Women's History Archive). 7 vols. Boston: G.K. Hall, 1975.

Ballou, Patricia. *Women: A Bibliography of Bibliographies.* 2d ed. Boston: G.K. Hall, 1987.

Berrian, Brenda F. *Bibliography of African Women Writers and Journalists: Ancient Egypt - 1984.* 1st ed. Washington, D.C.: Three Continents Press, 1985.

BiblioFem [microform]. London: Fawcett Library, City of London Polytechnic, 1978-1986.

Bibliography of American Women [microform]. New Haven: Research Publications, 198?.

Block, Adrienne Fried, and Carol Neuls-Bates. *Women in American Music: A Bibliography of Music and Literature.* Westport, CT: Greenwood Press, 1979.

Boos, Florence Saunders. *Bibliography of Women & Literature.* Janet Todd, editor. New York: Holmes & Meier, 1989. 2v.

Boxer, Marilyn. "For and About Women: The Theory and Practice of Women's Studies in the United States." *Signs* 7 (Spring 1982), pp. 662-695.

Bullwinkle, Davis. *African Women: A General Bibliography, 1976-1985.* Westport, CT: Greenwood Press, 1989.

Bullwinkle, Davis. *Women of Northern, Western, and Central Africa: A Bibliography, 1976-1985.* Westport, CT: Greenwood Press, 1989.

Byrne, Pamela. *Women in the Third World: A Historical Bibliography.* Santa Barbara, CA: ABC-Clio, 1986.

Capek, Mary Ellen S., ed. *A Women's Thesaurus: An Index of Language Used to Describe and Locate Information By and About Women.* New York: Harper & Row, 1987.

Catalogue of the Library of the International Archives for the Women's Movement (Interna-tionaal Archief voor de Vrouwenbeweging), Amsterdam. 4 v. Boston: G.K. Hall, 1980.

Chapman, Anne. *Feminist Resources for Schools and Colleges.* New York: Feminist Press, 1986.

Cheng, Lucie. *Women in China: Bibliography of Available English Language Materials.* Berkeley: Institute of East Asian Studies, University of California, 1984.

Cohen, Aaron I., comp. *International Discography of Women Composers.* Westport, CT: Greenwood Press, 1984.

Committee on the Status of Women in Librarianship. *Your Library: A Feminist Resource* [bibliographical pamphlets]. Chicago: COSWL, American Library Association, 1985.

Daims, Diva, and Janet Grimes. *Toward a Feminist Tradition: An Annotated Bibliography of Novels in English by Women, 1891-1920.* New York: Garland, 1982.

Danky, James P., Maureen Hady, et al, eds. *Women's Periodicals and Newspapers from the Eighteenth Century to 1981.* Boston: G.K. Hall, 1982.

Davis, Gwenn, and Beverly A. Joyce. *Personal Writings by Women to 1900: A Bibliography of American and British Writers.* Norman: University of Oklahoma Press, 1989.

Dickstein, Ruth, Victoria Mills, and Ellen Waite. *Women in LC's Terms: A Thesaurus of Library of Congress Subject Headings Relating to Women.* Phoenix: Oryx Press, 1988.

Dost, Jeanne, ed. *Women's Studies Bibliography, Kerr Library Collection.* Corvallis, OR: Women's Studies Program, Oregon State University, 1983.

Doughan, David, and Sanchez, Denise. *Feminist Periodicals, 1855-1984: An Annotated Critical Bibliography of British, Irish, Commonwealth and International Titles.* New York: New York University Press, 1987.

Feminist Periodicals: A Current Listing of Contents. Quarterly, 1981-. Madison: Office of the Women's Studies Librarian, University of Wisconsin.

Fenton, Thomas P., and Mary J. Heffron, eds. *Women in the Third World: A Directory of Resources.* Maryknoll, NY: Orbis Books, 1987.

Foster, Jeannette H. *Sex Variant Women in Literature.* Tallahassee, FL: Naiad Press, 1985 (originally published: New York: Vantage Press, 1956).

Frederiksen, Elke, ed. *Women Writers of Germany, Austria, and Switzerland: An Annotated Bio-Bibliographical Guide.* New York: Greenwood Press, 1989.

Frey, Linda, et al. *Women in Western European History.* 3 v. Westport, CT: Greenwood Press, 1982-.

The Gerritsen Collection of Women's History, 1543-1945 [microform]. Sanford, NC: Microfilming Corporation of America, 1975; now distributed by University Microfilms, Ann Arbor, MI. Two-volume printed guide edited by Duane R. Bogenschneider.

Grier, Barbara. *The Lesbian in Literature.* 3d ed. Tallahassee, FL: Naiad Press, 1981.

History of Women [microform]. New Haven: Research Publications, 1976. Accompanied by printed index.

Hunter College Women's Studies Collective, eds. *Women's Realities, Women's Choices: An Introduction to Women's Studies*. New York: Oxford University Press, 1983.

Ladyslipper Catalog and Resource Guide: Records and Tapes by Women. Ladyslipper, Inc., P.O. Box 3124, Durham, NC 27705.

Lehmann, Stephen and Eva Sartori, eds. *Women's Studies in Western Europe: A Resource Guide*. Chicago: American Library Association (ACRL), 1986.

Loeb, Catherine, Susan Searing, and Esther Stineman. *Women's Studies: A Recommended Core Bibliography, 1980-1985*. Littleton, CO: Libraries Unlimited, 1987.

Loeb, Catherine, Susan Searing, and Esther Stineman. *Women's Studies: A Recommended Core Bibliography, 1980-1985*. Abridged ed. Littleton, CO: Libraries Unlimited, 1987.

Mamola, Claire Zebroski. *Japanese Women Writers in English Translation: An Annotated Bibliography*. New York: Garland, 1989.

Marting, Diane E., ed. *Women Writers of Spanish America: An Annotated Bio-Bibliographical Guide*. New York: Greenwood Press, 1987.

Meghdessian, Samira Rafidi. *Status of the Arab Woman: A Select Bibliography*. Westport, CT: Greenwood Press, 1980.

Mehlman, Terry, ed. *Annotated Guide to Women's Periodicals in the United States and Canada*. Richmond, IN: Women's Programs Office, Earlham College, 1982-1985.

New Books on Women and Feminism. Semiannual. Madison: Office of the Women's Studies Librarian, University of Wisconsin.

Potter, Clare. *The Lesbian Periodicals Index*. Tallahassee, FL: Naiad Press, 1986.

Pritchard, Sarah. *Women's Studies Resources in Microform at the Library of Congress*. Washington, D.C.: General Reading Rooms Division, Library of Congress, 1985.

Przestwor, Joy C. *Connecting Women in the Community: A Handbook for Programs*. Cambridge, MA: Schlesinger Library, Radcliffe College, 1984.

Reardon, Joan, and Kristine Thorsen. *Poetry by American Women, 1900-1975: A Bibliography*. Metuchen, NJ: Scarecrow Press, 1979.

Reese, Lyn, and Jean Wilkinson, eds. *Women in the World: Annotated History Resources for the Secondary Student*. Metuchen, NJ: Scarecrow Press, 1987.

Resnick, Margery, and Isabelle de Courtivron. *Women Writers in Translation: An Annotated Bibliography, 1945-1982*. New York: Garland, 1984.

Rosenberg, Marie Barovic, and Len V. Bergstrom, eds. *Women and Society: A Critical Review of the Literature with a Selected Annotated Bibliography*. Beverly Hills: Sage, 1975. *Women and Society, citations 3601-6000*, edited by JoAnn Delores Een and Marie B. Rosenberg-Dishman. Beverly Hills: Sage, 1978.

Ruth, Sheila. *Issues in Feminism: A First Course in Women's Studies*. Boston: Houghton Mifflin, 1980.

Sakala, Carol. *Women of South Asia: A Guide to Resources*. New York: Kraus International Publications, 1980.

Schuster, Marilyn R., and Susan Van Dyne. *Women's Place in the Academy: Transforming the Liberal Arts Curriculum*. Totowa, N.J.: Rowman & Allanheld, 1985.

Schwartz, Narda Lacey. *Articles on Women Writers, 1976-1984: A Bibliography*. Santa Barbara: ABC-Clio, 1985. A prior volume covers 1960-1975.

Searing, Susan. *Introduction to Library Research in Women's Studies*. Boulder, CO: Westview Press,1985.

Simmons, Donita Vasiti. *Women in the South Pacific: A Bibliography*. Suva: University of the South Pacific Library, 1982.

Stimpson, Catharine, with Nina Kressner Cobb. *Women's Studies in the United States*. New York: Ford Foundation, 1986.

Stineman, Esther with Catherine Loeb. *Women's Studies: A Recommended Core Bibliography*. Littleton, CO: Libraries Unlimited, 1979.

Stoner, K. Lynn. *Latinas of the Americas: A Source Book*. New York: Garland, 1989.

Studies on Women Abstracts. 1983- . Oxfordshire, Eng.: Carfax Publ.

Sullivan, Kaye. *Films For, By, and About Women*. Metuchen, NJ: Scarecrow Press, 1980. *Films For, By, and About Women-- Series II*. Scarecrow, 1985.

Sveistrup, Hans, and Agnes Zahn-Harnack. *Die Frauenfrage in Deutschland: Stroemungen und Gegenstroemungen, 1790-1930*. Burg b.M.: A. Hopfer, 1934. Continued by *Die Frauenfrage in Deutschland: Bibliographie, 1931-1980*. Munich: K.G. Saur, 1982.

Terris, Virginia R. *Woman in America: A Guide to Information Sources*. Detroit: Gale, 1980.

Todd, Janet. *A Dictionary of British and American Women Writers, 1660-1800*. Totowa, NJ: Rowman & Allanheld, 1985.

Wei, Karen T. *Women in China: A Selected and Annotated Bibliography*. Westport, CT: Greenwood, 1984.

Women Studies Abstracts. 1972- . Rush, NY: Rush Publishing Co.

Yntema, Sharon. *More Than 100 Women Science Fiction Writers*. Freedom, CA: Crossing Press, 1988.

RLG CONSPECTUS©
Classification Lines for Women's Studies

Note: This is a consolidated list of the lines that apply to the women's studies Conspectus. Actual worksheets for completing Conspectus ratings and local notations are available from the Research Libraries Group. The worksheets reflect the integration of women's studies lines into the alphabetic grouping of existing Conspectus divisions, and incorporate line numbering specific to the Conspectus database structure (e.g., "AGR28.10" or "EDU131" for lines in parts of the agriculture or education divisions).

LC Class	Subject Group	Comments
B	Women in Philosophy	
B105.W6	Women philosophers	[philosophy of woman and of feminism: see HQ]
B187.W64	Ancient Greece - women philosophers	
BF	Women and psychology; women psychologists; women and psychoanalysis	
BF692, BF697.5.B63	Psychology - sex, sex differences; body image	[psychol. of women: also HQ]
BF1562-1584	Witchcraft	
BJ	Individual ethics - women - conduct of life; etiquette	[feminist ethics: see HQ]
BL-BX	Women and religion	
BL325	Comparative mythology - matriarchy, mother goddesses, virginity	
BL458	Women and religion	[see also HQ1393-1395]
BL473.5	Goddesses	
BL625.7	Women - religious life	
BM	Women in Judaism; women, Jewish	
BP	Women in Islam; women, Muslim	
BQ4570.W6	Women in Buddhism	
BR1713	Christianity - biography - women	

LC Class	Subject Group	Comments
BS575	Bible - biography - women and girls	
BS680.W7	Bible and women; Bible and feminism	[see also HQ1393-1395]
BS1199.W7	Bible - women in the Old Testament	
BS2417.W6	Bible - Jesus - attitude toward women	
BS2445, BS2545	Bible - women in the New Testament	
BT153.M6	God - attributes - motherhood - femininity	
BT590.W6	Christ - attitude toward women	
BT704	Theology - women; feminism and theology	[see also HQ1393-1395]
BV - BX	Women and Christianity	
BV639.W7	Church and women	
BV676	Women clergy	
BV2610-2612	Missionary work of women; women missionaries	
BV4395	Clergymen's wives	
BV4415	Women in church work	
BV4527	Women, Christian - religious life	
BV4844	Women - prayer-books and devotions	
BX1407.W65	Roman Catholic Church - history - U.S. - women	
BX1912.2	Roman Catholic Church - ordination of women; women priests	
BX2347.8.W6	Women in the Catholic Church	
BX4200-4556	Roman Catholic Church - nuns; monastic and religious life of women	
BX4656, BX4667	Catholic Church - biography - women, women saints	
BX5182, BX5185	Church of England - women, nuns	
BX5973-5974	Episcopal Church in the U.S. - religious orders of women	
BX7746, 7793	Women, Quaker	
BX8345.7, BX8493	Methodism - women	
BX8641	Mormons - women in mormonism	

LC Class	Subject Group	Comments
	<u>Biography and Genealogy of Women</u>	
C		
CT3200-3990	Biography of women - collective	[also in HQ1123]
D	<u>Women in History and War</u> (except the Americas)	
	[History of women by country: see HQ]	
D639.W7	World War, 1914-1918 - women	
D802, D810.W7	World War, 1939-1945 - women; women in underground and resistance movements	
DC145, DC158.8	France - Revolution, 1789-1799 - women	
DS559.8.W6	Vietnam - history - Vietnamese Conflict - women	
E	<u>Ethnic and Minority Women in North America; Women in U.S. Wars</u>	
	[History of women and feminism in the U.S.: see HQ]	
E98.W8	Indians of North America - women; Native American women	
E184	Mexican American women, Hispanic American women, Asian American women, Italian American women, ethnic women, etc. [women of ethnic groups are classed in E with that group, not in HQ]	
E185.86	Afro-American women	
E276	Revolution, 1775-1783 - women	
E628	Civil War, 1861-1865 - women	
G	<u>Women and Geography;</u> women–maps; women geographers	
GN-GT	<u>Anthropology, Customs and Folklore of Women</u>	
GN479	Anthropology - matriarchy; patriarchy; sex roles; women–social conditions	
GN482-484	Anthropology - life cycle: birth, adolescence, sexual behavior, marriage, bride price.	
GR470	Women - folklore	
GT	Costume	
GT3370	Widow burning (suttee)	

LC Class	Subject Group	Comments
<u>GV</u>	<u>Women and Sport</u>	
GV183, GV191	Women and recreation, outdoor recreation, women and wilderness	
GV362, GV439	Physical education for women and girls, women physical education teachers	
GV709, GV777-1061, 1111.5	Sports for women, self-defense for women	
<u>HA-HG</u>	<u>Women and Employment, Labor, Economics, and Finance</u>	
HD6050-6223	Women - employment	
HD6053-6059	General works; vocational guidance; occupational training; employment of married women, older women, minority women; women in business; women executives	
HD6060-6061	Sex discrimination in employment, sexual harassment, sexual division of labor; wages and salaries; equal pay for equal work.	
HD6064-6066	Hours, maternity leave	
HD6067	Occupational health and safety	
HD6068-6073	Industries and trades: factory labor, retail and service occupations, etc.	
HD6079	Women in trade-unions, labor movement	
HD6080	Women--pensions, social security	
HD6091-6220.7	Women--employment by region or country	
HD6095	Women--employment--U.S.	
HD6135	Women--employment--Great Britain	
HD6223	Women--employment--developing countries	
HD8039	Specific occupations: includes many female-dominated occupations (domestic servants, housewives/homemakers, secretaries, etc.)	
HF5549.5.A34	Affirmative action programs; employer-supported day care	
HF5500	Women executives	
HG8801, HG9291-9295	Women and life insurance, maternity insurance	
<u>HN-HV</u>	<u>Women and Sociology, Family, Sexuality; History of Women; Feminism</u>	
HN49.W6	Social history - women in social reform	

LC Class	Subject Group	Comments
HQ12-471	Sexual behavior	
	Sexual behavior of girls and women; sex education	
HQ27.5, HQ29, HQ46-51	Bisexuality, homosexuality, lesbianism	
HQ74-75	Prostitution, traffic in women, sex tourism	
HQ101-440		
HQ503-727	Family - history	
HQ759	Wives, mothers, surrogate mothers	
HQ763-766	Family planning - birth control	
HQ767	Abortion, sterilization	
HQ798	Female adolescence	
HQ800.2	Single women	
HQ998-999	Single mothers	
HQ1001-1043	Marriage	
HQ1075	Sex role, gender	
HQ1090	Men, male sex role, men's studies	
HQ1101-2030	Women, feminism	
HQ1101-1106	Periodicals, yearbooks, conferences	
HQ1115	Dictionaries, encyclopædias	
HQ1121-1122, 1399	Women, feminism--history, general	
HQ1123	Biography (collective)	[see also CT]
HQ1127-1139	History, primitive and ancient civilizations	
HQ1143-1149	History, medieval and renaissance	
HQ1150-1154	History, modern; 19th-20th cts.	
HQ1161-1172	Women, by broad ethnic groups (Muslim, Asian, Slavic, etc.)	[see also HQ1400+ by country]
	[for U.S. ethnic and minority women see E]	
HQ1180-1181	Women's studies	
HQ1201-1233	Women--general: feminism; psychology; philosophy; social conditions; sex role; life skills.	
	[Some numbers divided by language]	
HQ1236-1391	Women and the state; women in politics; women in public life;	
	women in development; women--economic conditions	
HQ1393-1395	Women and religion, women and the Bible; women's rights--religious aspects;	
	feminism--religious aspects	[see also B]
HQ1397	Women in science, in the professions; women scholars	

LC Class	Subject Group	Comments
HQ1400-1870.5	Women, feminism – [by region or country]	
HQ1402-1406	U.S. - periodicals, congresses, yearbooks	
HQ1410-1420	U.S. - history and biography	
HQ1423-1426	U.S. - reform literature; contemporary feminism; women--social conditions	
HQ1438-1439	U.S. - by states and cities	
HQ1451-1460	Canada	
HQ1460.5-HQ1525.95	Latin America (general), Central America, Caribbean	
HQ1526-1585	South America	
HQ1586-1725.5	Europe	
HQ1726-1735.2	Middle East	
HQ1735.3-1745.6	South Asia	
HQ1745.8-1760	Southeast Asia	
HQ1760.5-1781	Far East Asia	
HQ1784-1785	Arab and Islamic countries (collectively)	
HQ1786-1818.5	Africa	
HQ1821-1870.7	Australia, NZ, Oceania	
HQ1870.8	Communist countries (collectively)	
HQ1870.9	Developing countries (collectively)	
HQ1871-1885	Women's clubs - general works, history, periodicals	
HQ1901-2030.7	Women's clubs - by region or country	
HS3341-3365	Societies - girls' clubs, girl scouts and guides	
HV699-700	Maternal and infant welfare; family policy; single mothers; abused women	
HV851-859	Foster day care	
HV1442-1448	Social work with women	
HV1569, HV3021	Handicapped women	
HV6046	Female offenders, women criminals	
HV6250.4.W65	Violence against women; women victims of crime	
HV6558-6569	Rape	
HV6626	Wife abuse, battered women, battered wives	
HV8023	Policewomen	
HV8738, HV8836	Women prisoners	
HX546	Communism/socialism and women	

LC Class	Subject Group	Comments
J	Women in Government; Women's Political Rights [Women civil servants and woman suffrage are separately classed for each country. For general women in politics, see HQ1236-1391]	
JF847-855	Political rights and guaranties - women's suffrage (general)	
JK721	Women in the civil service - U.S.	
JK1880-1911	Politics, civil rights - women's suffrage - U.S.	
JL-JN	Women - suffrage; women in the civil service (other countries)	
JV6601.W7	Emigration and immigration - U.S. - women	
JX1965	Women and peace movements	
JX4211	Nationality, citizenship of women	
K	Women and Law [LC schedule for K is unfinished. Women's legal issues are classed by topic within each country; only U.S. is specified here.]	
K644	Comparative law - civil law - persons - women	
K675-K699	Civil law - family law - marriage	
K1772	Social legislation - labor law - discrimination - women	
K3243	Constitutional law - civil and political rights - sex discrimination	
K7155-7178	Conflict of laws - marriage and family	
KF	Women and law - United States	
KF299.W6	Women lawyers	
KF390.W6, KF478	Women - legal status, laws, etc; equal rights amendments	
KF3467, KF3555	Women - employment - law and legislation	
KF4758	Constitutional law - civil rights - sex discrimination	
KF4895	Constitutional law - suffrage - women	
KF9315	Criminal law - abortion	
KF9329	Criminal law - rape	

LC Class	Subject Group	Comments
L		
	Women and Education	
LB2332.3	Higher education - women teachers, professors	
LB2837	School administration - women teachers	
LB3045.66	School administration - textbooks - sexism	
LB3433	Adolescent pregnancy	
LC212.8-.863	Sex discrimination in education	
LC1401-2571	Education of women	
LC1411-1426	General works	
LC1421-1466	Early works to 1870	
LC1481-1486	General works, 1871-	
LC1496	Nonformal education	
LC1500-1506	Vocational education	
LC1551-1651	Higher education of women, coeducation	
LC1660-1666	Adult education	
LC1701-2571	History - by region and country:	
LC1701-1707	General	
LC1751-1759	United States	
LC1761-1769	Canada	
LC1771-1909	Central America and Caribbean	
LC1911-2029	South America	
LC2031-2300	Europe	
LC2301-2410	Asia	
LC2411-2471	Africa	
LC2481-2571	Australia, NZ, Oceania	
LD7020-7251	Women's colleges and girls' schools in the U.S.	
LE-LG	Women's colleges and girls' schools - by country	
LJ141-145	Sororities and women's fraternities	

LC Class	Subject Group	Comments
M	Women and Music	
M1664.W8, M1665.W8	National music - U.S. - women's suffrage movement	
M1952-M1956	Women's college songs	
M1977-M1978	Songs on special topics - women, housewives, mothers, etc.	
ML	Women composers, women musicians	[not classed together]
ML82	Women and music, feminism and music	
ML128.W7	Music - bibliography - women in music	
ML156.4.W6	Music - bibliography - discography - women in music	
N	Women in Art	
N43	Visual arts - biography - women artists	
N72.F45	Visual arts and feminism	
N7630-7639	Women in art - feminism, beauty (aesthetics)	
N8345	Visual arts as a profession - women artists	
NA1997	Women architects	
NC1763.W6	Caricature - special subjects - women	
ND	Women painters	
NK	Women and design, women designers	
NX164.W65	The arts (in general) as a profession - women in the arts	
NX180.F4	The arts (in general) - feminism and the arts	
NX652.W6	Characters or people in art - women	

LC Class	Subject Group	Comments
P	Women and Language, Literature, and Mass Media	
	[Does not include individual literary works, or criticism on individual authors.]	
P94.5.W65, P96.S45, .S48, .S5	Communication - mass media and women, sex, sexism, sex roles, pornography	
P120.S48	Linguistic theory - sex differences, sexism in language	
PA	Women in Greek and Latin literature	
PG2989.W6	Russian literature - women in literature	
PG2997	Russian literature - women authors	
PG3015, 3026, 3096	Russian literature - 19th and 20th cent. - women in literature	
PG3203-3235	Russian literature - collections - women, women authors	
PL	Women in Asian literature	
PL722, PL725	Japanese literature - women	
PL957, PL973, PL975	Korean literature - women	
PL2275, PL2278, PL2515	Chinese literature - women	
PN56.L45, .S52, .W7	Literary theory - special subjects - lesbianism, sex role, women and poets	
PN56.5.W64	Literary theory - characters - women	
PN98.W64	Literary criticism - women as critics - feminist criticism	
PN471-479	Literary history - biography - women authors	
PN682.W6	Literary history - medieval - women	
PN810.W66	Literary history - romance literatures - women	
PN1009.5.S48	Folk literature - juvenile literature - sexism, sex roles	
PN1024	Poetry by women	
PN1091	Women and poetry - feminine influence	
PN1590.W64	Performing arts - women in the performing arts	
PN1992.8.W65	Broadcasting - women in television, feminism and television	
PN1995.9.W6	Women in film and motion pictures; feminism and motion pictures; women motion picture producers.	
PN2270.F45	Drama - U.S. - feminist theater	
PN2595.13.W65	Drama - Gr. Brit. - feminist theater	
PN3160.W64	Drama - amateur theatricals - women	

LC Class	Subject Group	Comments
PN3401	Prose fiction - women writers - feminism in fiction	
PN4193.W7	Oratory - women speakers	
PN4784.W7, 4872	Journalism - women in journalism, biography	
PN4879	Journalism - U.S. - women's magazines	
PN4888.W65	Journalism - portrayal of women in the press	
PN5124.W6	Women's periodicals, English	
PN6069.W65	Collections of general literature - women authors	
PN6071.W7	Collections of general literature - by subject - women	
PN6081.5, 6084.W6	Collections of quotations - women authors, women	
PN6109.9, 6110.W6	Collections of poetry - women authors, women	
PN6120.W6	Collections of drama - women	
PN6231.F44, .W6	Collections of wit and humor - feminism, women	
PQ	Women in Romance literature	
PQ145, 155, 295, 637	French literature - history - women in literature	
PQ149, 307, 1107, 1167	French literature - history, collections - women authors, women poets	
PQ3823.W6	French literature outside France - women authors	
PQ4053.W6, 4055.W6	Italian literature - history - women authors, women in literature	
PQ6048.W6 - PQ6177	Spanish literature - history, collections - women authors, women poets, women in literature	
	(see PQ6055, 6098.W64, 6140.W6, 6177)	
PQ7133-PQ9653	Latin American literature - women, women authors, women poets	
PR	Women in English literature	
PR111-116, 119, 151.W6, 409.W65	English literature - history - women authors, women in literature	
PR429.W64	English literature - history - Elizabethan - women	
PR448.W65	English literature - history - 18th cent. - women authors	
PR468.W6, 469.W65	English literature - history - 19th cent. - women, women authors	
PR508.W6, 535.W58, 535.W6	English literature - history - poetry - women, women authors	
PR635.W6, .W62	English literature - history - drama - women, women authors	
PR658.S42, .W6, 698.W6	English literature - history - drama - Elizabethan and Restoration - sex role, women	
PR830.W6	English literature - history - novel - women	
PR1110.W6	English literature - collections - women authors	
PR1111.F45, .W6	English literature - collections - periodicals - feminism, women	
PR1195.F45, .W6	English literature - collections - poetry - feminism, women	
PR1246.W65	English literature - collections - drama - women authors	
PR1286.W6, 1309.W7	English literature - collections - prose - women authors, women	

LC Class	Subject Group	Comments
PS	**Women in American literature**	
PS147-152	American literature - history - women authors	
PS217.W64	American literature - history - 19th cent. - women	
PS228.W65	American literature - history - 20th cent. - women	
PS310.F45	American literature - history - poetry - feminism	
PS338.W6	American literature - history - drama - women	
PS374.F45, .W6	American literature - history - fiction - feminism, women	
PS508.W7	American literature - collections - women authors	
PS509.F44, .L47, .W6	American literature - collections - feminism, lesbianism, women	
PS589	American literature - collections - women poets	
PS595.L46	American literature - collections - poetry - lesbianism	
PS627.W66, 628.W6	American literature - collections - drama - women, women authors	
PS647-648	American literature - collections - prose - women authors, feminism, lesbianism, women	
PT	**Women in Germanic literature**	
PT151.W7, 167	German literature - history - women in literature, women authors	
PT1107, 1109-1110, 1156, 1352	German literature - collections - women, women authors, women poets, women's letters	
PT5085-PT9556	Dutch and Scandinavian literatures - women, women authors, feminism	
Q	**Women in Mathematics; Women and Science**	
Q130, Q181	Women in science, women scientists, feminism and science education	
QA27.5	Women in mathematics, women mathematicians	
QP		
QP34.5	Women and biology, physiology; sexism and sociobiology	
QP251	Women–physiology; sex differences	
	Reproductive technology	
QP259-265	Reproduction - female sex physiology	
QP285	Reproduction - physiology - parturition, birth	

LC Class	Subject Group	Comments
R		
	Women and Medicine	
R692	Women in medicine, women physicians, sexism in medicine	
RA564.85	Public health - women's health services	
RA778	Women - health and hygiene - handbooks, guides	
RC451.4.W6, 455.5.S45	Psychiatry - women, sex roles	
RC489.F45	Psychiatry - feminist therapy	
RC552.A5, .B84	Psychiatry - anorexia nervosa, bulimia	
RC569.5.F3	Psychiatry - wife abuse, abuse of women	
RC963.6.W65	Industrial medicine and hygiene - women; occupational health	
RC1218.W65	Sports medicine - women	
RG1-991	**Gynecology and obstetrics**	
RG1-47	General and collected works	
RG12-16	Hospitals, clinics, etc. for women; feminist health clinics	
RG51-76	History, biography	
RG121-123	Popular works; addresses, essays, lectures	
RG125-131	Therapeutics	
RG133-138	Conception; fertilization in vitro; contraception	
RG141-149	Study and teaching	
RG159-499	Female diseases and systemic disorders; endocrine gynecology; menstrual disorders; menopause; infertility; diseases of the genital organs, breast disease.	
	Obstetrics	
RG500-991	History, biography	
RG509-518	General and popular works	
RG521-525	Pregnancy, labor, abortion	
RG551-791	Maternal care; midwives; childbirth education	
RG940-991		
RT1-120	**Nursing**	
RT4-5	United States (general)	
RT6-8	Canada, Central and South America	
RT10-12	Europe	
RT13-17	Asia, Africa, Australia and New Zealand, Pacific Islands	
RT21-29	General, employment, communication, statistics	

LC Class	Subject Group	Comments
	(Nursing)	
RT31-41	History and biography; general works	
RT69-81	Nursing education	
RT82-84	Nursing personnel, vocational guidance, men and minorities	
RT85-86	Nursing ethics, psychology, social aspects, sexism	
S	Women and Agriculture: women farmers	
	[Women in agricultural work: see HD6073]	
S518	Agricultural handbooks for women	
T	Women and Technology	
T36	Women in technology; women inventors	
TR	Women and Photography: women photographers; photography of women	
TX1-TX840	Home economics	
TX15-19	History	
TX21-126	By country	
TX139-140	Biography	
TX144-150	General works	
TX151-162	Handbooks of home economics	
TX164-286	Home economics as a profession, home economics study and teaching	
TX301-339	Housekeeping, household management; interior decoration; consumer education	
TX361.W55, .W7	Nutrition - women, working women	
TX645-840	Cookery	

LC Class	Subject Group	Comments
U-V		
U21.75	War - military sociology - women and the military	
UA45	Armies - U.S. - Armed Forces women's reserves	
UA565.W6	Armies - U.S. - Women's Army Corps	
UB416-419	Military - U.S. - women in the armed forces, women soldiers	
UH	Army nurses, military nursing	
V		
VA390.S6, 390.W3, 324.W65	Navy - U.S. - Coast Guard Women's Reserve, Navy Women's Reserves (WAVES), women in the navy	
VE23.4	U.S. Marine Corps - women's reserve	
VG350-355	Nurse corps	
Z	Women in Publishing; Library science; Bibliography	
Z286.F45	Bookselling and publishing - feminist literature	
Z682.4.W65	Women in librarianship	
Z688.W65; Z711.92.W65	Library collections - women's studies, reference books on women	
Z1039.W65	Books for special classes - women	
Z1209.2	Indians of North America - women, Native American women	
Z1229.W8	National bibliography - American literature - women authors	
Z1361	Afro-American women, Mexican American women, ethnic women	
Z2013.5.W6	National bibliography - English literature - women authors	
Z5703.4.R35, .W53	Rape, violence against women, abuse	
Z5775-5777	Home economics	
Z5917.W6	Fiction - women authors	
Z5983.W65	Folklore - women	
Z6514.C5W64-W648	Literature - characters, themes, etc. - women	
Z6671	Gynecology and obstetrics; abortion	
Z7164	Political and social sciences: birth control, marriage, pornography, sex, homosexuality, single mothers, etc.	
Z7961-7965	Women, feminism	